# Methods of
# *Persuasion*

# Methods of
## *Persuasion*

HOW TO USE PSYCHOLOGY TO
INFLUENCE HUMAN BEHAVIOR

*Nick Kolenda*

*Methods of Persuasion: How to Use Psychology to Influence Human Behavior*
Copyright 2013 © Kolenda Group, LLC
www.NickKolenda.com

ISBN: 0615815650
ISBN-13: 9780615815657

# Table of Contents

# Acknowledgments

Researchers are somewhat unlucky. Many work their butts off to expand our knowledge of human behavior, yet the majority of those researchers remain unknown and unrecognized.

Though they're under tremendous pressure to "publish or perish," researchers are pressured to publish their work in top-level academic journals (journals that you'll be hard-pressed to find in any mainstream household). In fact, researchers who publish their work in a book for the general public are sometimes viewed as a "sellout," so it seems like many researchers are destined to remain unknown because of those unfortunate circumstances.

Accordingly, I'd like to acknowledge all of the researchers who *are* helping to further our understanding of human behavior. In particular, I want to acknowledge the researchers whose work sparked my own interest in this pursuit: Robert Cialdini, Daniel Kahneman, Dan Ariely, John Bargh, Gavan Fitzsimons, Richard Petty, John Cacioppo, Leon Festinger, Ap Dijksterhuis, and the list goes on. Your work is truly revolutionary, and you deserve the utmost recognition and praise.

# Preface

Let me guess. You skipped over the Acknowledgments and came directly to the Preface, right? Most people do. If you *are* among that majority, go back and read the Acknowledgments, and then come back here.

Are you back? Great. My name is Nick Kolenda, and I've been a professional mind reader for 10 years. Do I have supernatural powers? Nope. Just a pretty good knack at reading people and influencing their thoughts.

As a mind reader, I've structured my entire performance around the concept of psychological influence, and over the course of 10 years, I developed a unique method to unconsciously influence people's thoughts. Where does the "mind reading" come into play? Because those people are unaware that I influenced their thoughts, I can reveal the thought that I implanted and, essentially, "read their mind." I've always kept my method hidden, but this book finally reveals that explanation (and the psychology behind why it works).

But this book stems far beyond that one mind reading application. Not only will *Methods of Persuasion* teach you how to influence people's thoughts, but it will also teach you how to use psychology to control their behavior. In addition to my unique background as a mind reader, I also have an educational background in persuasion through my degrees in marketing and psychology. While in college, I became obsessed with finding the psychological forces that guide human behavior, and although most people can barely make it through one scholarly article, I sifted through hundreds—if not thousands—of academic journal articles, trying to pinpoint proven principles that guide our behavior.

In my pursuit, I discovered several psychological forces that exert an incredibly powerful influence on our behavior. These principles are so pervasive and ingrained within us that they guide our behavior every day without our conscious awareness. More importantly, if you know how to alter those forces, you can use them to guide people's behavior.

This book will teach you those principles and more.

Best wishes,


Nick Kolenda
October, 2013

# Introduction

Humans are marionettes. Attached to each of us are sets of strings that, when pulled in a certain direction, guide our behavior without our awareness. If you know how to control the strings, then you know how to control behavior. This book teaches you how to control those strings. *This book will teach you how to successfully (and ethically) become a puppeteer in a world full of human marionettes.*

Because of my peculiar background as a mind reader and psychology researcher, the book that you're holding is pretty unique. But there's one particular distinction that makes it especially different from other books on persuasion. Most persuasion books simply list an arsenal of tactics that you can use at your disposal; however, the persuasion methods in this book have been strategically arranged into a chronological seven-step process. If you need to persuade someone to perform a specific task, you can follow the exact steps described in this book to achieve your goal. Although you can still pick and choose the persuasion tactics that you want to implement, this step-by-step guide will get you headed in the right direction.

Conveniently, this step-by-step persuasion process follows the acronym METHODS (do you get the book title's double entendre?). The overall steps in METHODS include:

- ➢ Step 1: Mold Their Perception
- ➢ Step 2: Elicit Congruent Attitudes
- ➢ Step 3: Trigger Social Pressure
- ➢ Step 4: Habituate Your Message
- ➢ Step 5: Optimize Your Message
- ➢ Step 6: Drive Their Momentum
- ➢ Step 7: Sustain Their Compliance

It might seem like a simple list, but the amount of psychology litera-ture that I scoured to produce that list is mind-numbing (feel free to take a gander at the list of references at the end of the book).

Part of my goal in writing this book was to make it the book in your collection with the most highlighting. You won't find any long-winded explanations, irrelevant anecdotes, or any other type of "fluff" because I've tried to make everything as direct and straight to the point as possible (while still making the book interesting and engag-ing to read).

**Last-Minute Background Info.** Before jumping straight to the first step in METHODS, there's some last-minute background information that can help you gain the most from reading this book.

*Persuasion Is Not Manipulation.* The term "manipulation" generally refers to a malicious attempt to influence another person through questionable or blatantly unethical tactics (e.g., lying and deceit). The term "persuasion" is sometimes grouped with "manipulation," which is very unfortunate because the two terms represent very different ideas.

The tactics in this book are neither ethical nor unethical; *how you use these tactics* will determine that outcome. Although it's not my job to "persuade" you to adopt a moral outlook, I wholeheartedly oppose any-one who tries to use these tactics to manipulate people. The principles in this book can be very powerful, and I urge everyone to use them with proper care and concern for other people. You should never try to persuade people to perform actions if you know that those actions are not in their best interest.

*Definitions.* In this book, I'll use the term "target" when referring to the person(s) that you're trying to persuade. For example, if you're trying to persuade a coworker to write you a recommendation, your coworker would be your "target" (you should also note that I will ran-domly alternate between using "he" and "she" pronouns when refer-ring to a hypothetical person).

I'll also use the term "request" when you're trying to persuade someone to perform a specific behavior (e.g., to write a recommendation), and I'll use the term "message" when referring to the medium that you use for persuasion (e.g., an e-mail to your coworker). But both terms will be used more or less interchangeably.

Lastly, most of the techniques in this book exert a "nonconscious" influence, meaning that people will be unaware that those principles are guiding their behavior. In writing this book, I chose to use the word "nonconscious" because the terms "subconscious" and "unconscious" have a connotation that there's some part of our brain responsible for unconscious processes (which isn't the case). The term "nonconscious" seems more accurate because it makes no such claim; it just refers to everything that occurs outside of our awareness.

*Structure of Chapters.* The book is divided into seven parts, with each part representing a step in the METHODS process. Each of those seven parts will contain several chapters that explain a relevant psychological principle that you can use to accomplish the overarching step.

Every chapter in this book shares a similar structure. I'll first describe the background of the principle and how it exerts its influence in our daily lives. Next, I'll describe the psychology research to explain why that principle is so powerful. Lastly, each chapter will end with various example strategies to apply that principle toward persuasion.

If I'm so committed to being clear and concise, why am I bothering to teach the underlying psychology? Why not focus solely on the applications? There are two main reasons. First, by citing the research to support the principle, I'm hoping that you can gain an appreciation for the effectiveness of each application. Second, and more importantly, in order to take full advantage of the *how,* you need to understand the *why.* Once you understand the underlying psychology, you can start to move beyond the example techniques that I describe, and you can start to brainstorm your own persuasion applications and strategies. It's like the Chinese proverb: Give a man a fish and you feed him for a day; teach a man to fish and you feed him for a lifetime.

# STEP 1

# Mold Their Perception

| | Step 1: | **M** | **Mold Their Perception** |
|---|---|---|---|
| **Before the Request** | Step 2: | **E** | Elicit Congruent Attitudes |
| | Step 3: | **T** | Trigger Social Pressure |
| | Step 4: | **H** | Habituate Your Message |
| **During the Request** | Step 5: | **O** | Optimize Your Message |
| | Step 6: | **D** | Drive Their Momentum |
| **After the Request** | Step 7: | **S** | Sustain Their Compliance |

## OVERVIEW:
## MOLD THEIR PERCEPTION

Reality is objective, but our perception of reality is subjective. What the heck does that mean? Even though there's only one reality surrounding us, people perceive and interpret that reality differently. Essentially, our perception is a lens through which we interpret reality; if you know how to alter that lens, you can change how people view and interpret reality.

That notion leads to the most common error in persuasion. When people need to persuade someone to comply with a request, they usually jump straight to the request without devoting attention to possible strategies leading up to that request. People start relentlessly hammering away, trying to extract their target's compliance, unbeknownst to them that they could have used a few psychological tactics to change how their target would perceive their request.

Accordingly, the chapters in this first step will teach you how to alter the lens through which people perceive the world around them, and you'll learn how to mold their perception so that it becomes more conducive to your situation. Once you alter that lens, any additional persuasion tactics will become much more powerful and effective because of their new perception. The first chapter starts by describing one of the most important factors that dictates our perception: our current mindset.

# CHAPTER 1

# Prime Their Mindset

It might seem like an odd request, but think of a lucky dwarf. Are you thinking of one? Good. Now go with your immediate gut reaction and think of a number between one and ten. Quick! Stick with the first number that pops inside your head, and don't change your mind.

Are you thinking of a number? Although it's far from foolproof, you were more likely to think of the number seven. And if you *are* thinking of seven and you're somewhat freaked out, rest assured, this chapter will explain the psychological principle behind that phenomenon. Specifically, you'll learn why imagining that "lucky dwarf" made you more likely to think of the number seven, and you'll learn practical techniques to apply that underlying principle in your own life (don't worry, you won't be asking people to think about dwarves, I promise).

## THE POWER OF MINDSETS

Before I explain the exercise with the dwarf, let's try something else. This time, think of your mother. Let that image of good ol' mum simmer for a second or two, and then let it fade away.

Now, read the following blurb about Mark and mentally rate his level of motivation on a scale from one to nine (1 = low motivation, 9 = high motivation):

> Mark is just entering his second year of college. In his first year, he did very well in some classes but not as well in others. Although he missed some morning classes, overall he had very good attendance. His parents are both doctors, and he is registered in pre-med, but he

hasn't really decided if that is what he wants to do.
(Fitzsimons & Bargh, 2003, p. 153)

Do you have your rating? As you might have judged, all of the information about Mark in that passage was completely ambiguous; in other words, that information could be perceived either positively or negatively. Researchers presented that ambiguous blurb to people to examine how their perception of Mark would change depending on their mindset.

To instill a certain mindset in their participants, the researchers asked people beforehand to complete an "unrelated" questionnaire. Some people completed a questionnaire about their best friend, whereas other people completed a questionnaire about their mother.

Do you still remember the rating that you gave Mark? The people in the study who filled out the best friend questionnaire gave an average rating of 5.56 for Mark's level of motivation. Was your rating higher? According to the results, people who filled out the questionnaire about their mother viewed Mark to be significantly more motivated (Fitzsimons & Bargh, 2003).

Why did people perceive Mark differently depending on the questionnaire? Since nothing in the blurb changed, logic suggests that both groups should have given Mark the same rating. What was so powerful about the mother questionnaire that altered people's perception of him?

In general, people associate motivation and striving toward success more with their mothers than with their best friends. Because one of the driving forces behind many people's pursuit toward success is a desire to make their mom proud, the concept of motivation became activated and more prevalent for people who completed the questionnaire about their mother. Although the objective reality in front of them remained the same (i.e., the blurb was the same for each group), the idea of "mother" became a lens through which people perceived that ambiguous blurb. The next section will explain why that's the case, and you'll also learn why a "lucky dwarf" can make people predisposed to think of the number seven.

## WHY ARE MINDSETS SO POWERFUL?

To understand why mindsets are so powerful, you need to understand three concepts: schemas, priming, and spreading activation.

**Schemas.** For any general concept, you usually associate many other ideas with that concept. For example, your concept of mother would include the idea of motivation, along with many other ideas that you associate with your mother.

Further, if that set of associations—known as a *schema*—becomes activated, it can alter your perception and behavior because it would make the other associated concepts more prevalent in your mind (e.g., activating a schema of mother made the idea of motivation more prevalent, which influenced people's perception of Mark).

Though schemas can often result in positive perceptions, such as perceived motivation, schemas can also result in negative perceptions, such as stereotypes. For example, under your schema of "Asian" is probably the idea of superior math skills. Even if you don't believe that Asians are genuinely superior at math, the mere presence of that association is enough to influence your perception and behavior.

Researchers from Harvard conducted a clever study to test that claim (Shih, Pittinsky, & Ambady, 1999). Their study was particularly clever because they used a group of people who belonged to conflicting stereotypes: Asian-American women. On one hand, there's a common stereotype that Asians are superior at math, but on the other hand, there's a common stereotype that females are inferior at math. The researchers wanted to examine how activating those conflicting schemas could influence their performance on a math test.

Before giving the test, the researchers asked two groups of Asian-American women some questions. Some women were asked questions that related to their sex (e.g., if the floors in their dorms were either co-ed or single sex). Other women, however, were asked questions that related to their race and heritage (e.g., the languages that they knew or spoke at home). Thus, one group had their schema of "female" activated, whereas the other group had their schema of "Asian" activated. You can probably guess what happened when the researchers later presented those groups with a supposedly unrelated math test.

Women who were primed with their schema for Asian performed significantly better than a control group (women who were asked neutral questions), and women who were primed with their schema for female performed significantly worse than the control group. Therefore, any idea that we associate with a particular schema—even if we don't believe in that association—can still influence our perception and behavior if that schema becomes activated.

But how does a schema become activated in the first place? The answer lies in priming.

**Priming.** *Priming* is the means by which you activate a schema or mindset. In the previous study about stereotypes, the "prime" was the questionnaire. When people filled out the questionnaire, their schema for either Asian or female became activated.

Does that mean you need to ask people to complete a questionnaire in order to prime a schema? Nope. Luckily, there are many easier ways to prime particular schemas (though I suppose you *could* ask your target to fill out a questionnaire if you really wanted to).

If not by questionnaire, how else can you prime a schema? Research shows that you can prime a schema by merely exposing people to certain words or ideas related to a particular schema. To illustrate, the next study offers a prime example (ha, get the pun?).

Using the disguise of a word-puzzle task, Bargh, Chen, and Burrows (1996) exposed people to words relating to the elderly (e.g., *bingo, wise, retired, Florida*). When the experiment was supposedly over, what do you think happened when people walked out of the room? Astonishingly, compared to a control group, people walked out of the room significantly slower when they were exposed to the elderly related words. Those words primed a schema for the elderly, which then activated behavior that people associate with the elderly: walking slow.

Not only can priming occur through subtle exposures to certain words, but priming can also be effective when it occurs entirely outside of our conscious awareness. Researchers in another study subliminally primed people with either the logo from Apple, a company with a very creative connotation, or the logo from IBM, a company with a very straightforward, noncreative connotation. The logos were only shown for thirteen milliseconds, so people weren't consciously aware that they were exposed to those logos. However, people who were flashed with Apple's logo exhibited higher creativity than did people who were exposed to IBM's logo (Fitzsimons, Chartrand, & Fitzsimons, 2008).

How was creativity measured? After subliminally priming people with the logos, the researchers asked them to list unusual uses for a brick. Yep . . . a brick. It might seem like a silly task, but people who were subliminally primed with Apple's logo generated a significantly longer list than those primed with IBM's logo. Even the unusual uses themselves were judged to be more creative than the uses generated from the IBM group. Therefore, priming is very effective even when it occurs outside of our conscious awareness.

Although it should be clear by now that priming a particular schema can influence our perception and behavior, *why* is that the case? The answer lies in spreading activation.

**Spreading Activation.** Our brains have a semantic network, a giant interconnected web of knowledge containing everything that we've learned over time. Each concept in that network, referred to as a "node," is connected to other concepts that are related in some aspect (the more related they are, the stronger the connection that exists between them). Due to those connections, whenever a node in our semantic network becomes activated (via some type of prime), all other nodes that are connected become activated as well, a principle known as *spreading activation* (Collins & Loftus, 1975).

Remember the lucky dwarf from the beginning of the chapter? Spreading activation can explain why thinking about that statement can make people more likely to choose the number seven. Essentially, the number seven is a node in our semantic network, and it has connections to other nodes. For most people, a node of the number seven would have connections to things like seven deadly sins, 7-UP soda, the Seven Wonders of the World, and an unfathomable number of other related associations. But why does a "lucky dwarf" activate the idea of seven? It combines two other ideas that are heavily associated with seven: "lucky number seven" and *Snow White and the Seven Dwarves*.

Due to the connections that exist between those two concepts and the number seven in our brain's semantic network, mentioning those concepts can trigger spreading activation. When those two nodes become activated, the activation spreads to the number seven node, which makes it more readily available on a nonconscious level. If you're forced to choose the first number that pops into your head, you're more likely to choose the number seven because it will come to your mind more easily.

Further, you would have been even more likely to choose the number seven if I had casually mentioned other concepts relating to the number seven, perhaps about a "deadly sin" or lemon-lime soda. Those comments would have activated more concepts connected to the node of the number seven, which would have increased the strength of the spreading activation. At the end of this chapter, I'll describe how I accomplish some of my mind reading feats using that same principle.

But first, the next section will teach you how to take advantage of schemas, priming, and spreading activation to prime a favorable mindset in your persuasion target (the terms "schema" and "mindset" are fairly similar, so they'll be used interchangeably throughout this chapter).

## PERSUASION STRATEGY: PRIME THEIR MINDSET

Up to this point, the chapter has explained how priming a particular schema can trigger spreading activation. This section will expand that knowledge by describing some specific schemas that *would* be favorable for you to activate in your target.

**Prime Their Perception.** Our perception of the world is largely dictated by the primes in our surrounding environment. For example, experienced advertisers realize that choosing when and where to air a television commercial is an extremely important choice because of priming effects. When viewers watch the last scene before a commercial break, that last scene can activate a certain schema, which can then influence how people perceive the next commercial. Similar to how activating a schema of mother can influence how people perceived an ambiguous situation, certain scenes before a commercial break can activate schemas that will influence how people perceive commercials.

Consider the television show, *Grey's Anatomy*. Nearly every scene before a commercial break in *Grey's Anatomy* ends on a depressing cliffhanger. A likable main character just discovers the terrible news that she has cancer and is going to die within three months. *Bam!* Commercial break.

Choosing to air your commercial at this exact moment would be a horrible marketing strategy (unless your product is life insurance, perhaps). For one, viewers are likely to associate their depressed feelings with your product because of classical conditioning (explained in Chapter 14). More broadly, however, that depressing scene will activate a schema of sadness, hopelessness, or some other negative schema through which viewers will perceive and interpret your commercial. To avoid that negative association and detrimental schema, advertisers should avoid airing their commercial after harmful exposures, and instead, strive to position their commercial after favorable exposures (some favorable exposures will be explained later in this section).

Priming effects occur outside of advertising as well. Whether you're giving a speech, writing a school essay, or even showing your spouse your new haircut, we experience instances each day where we want our message to be perceived in the best possible light. This section will explain one type of schema that you can activate in all situations, and you'll also learn other types of favorable schemas that you can activate depending on the situation.

*Standard Schema.* If you want to trigger a more open-minded perception in your target, why not simply prime a schema of open-mindedness? In fact, exposure to words merely relating to open-mindedness (e.g., *flexible, elastic, rubber, change*) have been found to trigger more open-minded perceptions (Hassin, 2008). Bingo!

And there's even more good news. Although it wouldn't hurt to mention your "flexible" schedule, there's an even simpler way to activate an open-minded schema. The studies in this chapter have shown that you can easily activate schemas by simply getting someone to think about a concept. To activate an open-minded perception, you simply need to expose your target to an example of open-mindedness.

One simple technique to activate an open-minded perception is to initiate a conversation that revolves around the idea of open-mindedness. Perhaps a few minutes before you present your message or make your request, you casually describe a story of someone who recently tried a new experience and enjoyed it. Even something as simple as the following can work:

➤ Remember how you told me that I should start listening to the band, Mumford & Sons? I didn't like them at first, but I listened to them again, and I really like them now.

Making a simple and innocent statement about someone acting open-mindedly can help activate your target's schema of open-mindedness, and that activation will trigger a more open-minded perception. Much like asking people to think about their mother can cause them to perceive someone as more motivated, getting someone to think about open-mindedness will create a lens through which they will perceive things from a more open-minded perspective.

And if the previous conversation starter doesn't suit your personality or the situation, no worries! There are plenty of other conversation starters that you can use:

➤ What are your thoughts on skydiving? My friend Sandra was petrified about going, but she recently went, and she absolutely loved it.

➤ Do you like eggplant? My friend Bill used to hate eggplant with a passion, but he recently tried it and, it's funny, he actually loves it now. I've never been a huge fan of eggplant, but I guess I'll have to try it again sometime.

➤ My company just hired a new employee. Although I didn't like him at first, I kept an open mind, and he's finally starting to grow on me.

I'm not suggesting that you should lie, but rather, you should try to think of a genuine conversation piece that would revolve around the idea of open-mindedness. The more detailed and elaborate the conversation, the stronger you activate someone's schema for open-mindedness, which will then trigger a more favorable perception of your message.

And if you can't think of something relating to open-mindedness, you can still take advantage of this concept by activating other schemas that can still be very favorable for your situation. The next section explains some of those schemas.

*Other Schemas.* One of the great benefits about priming is its versatility. Because of spreading activation, there are plenty of other effective schemas that you can activate to make your request seem more appealing.

Suppose that you're placing an advertisement in a magazine to promote a book that you wrote on persuasion (pfft, who writes books on persuasion—that's lame). When you speak with the editor or representative about your ad placement, you ask her to describe a few of the article topics that will appear in the issue, and you discover that one of the articles will describe an interview conducted with an author whose book recently became a bestseller.

As the devious persuader that you are, you decide to take advantage of the opportunity. You realize that the interview will prime magazine readers with a "bestseller" schema, and so you decide to purchase a full page ad for your book on the page immediately after the interview with the bestselling author. Even though readers will consciously recognize that you're not the same author described in the interview on the previous page, they're likely to perceive your book more favorably because a "bestseller" schema will have become activated. As a result, you'll persuade a larger percentage of people to purchase your book than you would have persuaded by randomly choosing an ad placement.

**Prime Their Behavior.** What if, instead of perception, you wanted to trigger compliance toward a request? In these situations that rely more on behavior, priming the concept of open-mindedness might not do the trick. So are you out of luck? Nope. You simply need to prime a different mindset.

Remember how elderly words activated people's schema for the elderly and caused them to walk more slowly? Mounting research has shown that a variety of different behaviors can be triggered through priming. To see the endless potential of priming, take a look at Table 1.1 to see some interesting findings that other research has found.

| Table 1.1 Priming Effects on Behavior | | |
|---|---|---|
| **Mindset** | **Prime** | **Outcome** |
| Politeness[1] | Exposure to words about politeness (e.g., *respect, honor, considerate*) | People waited significantly longer before interrupting an experimenter |
| Friendship[2] | A questionnaire about a friend | People were more likely to assist in a follow-up research study |
| Intellect[3] | People were asked to write a short essay about college professors | People answered more questions correctly in a game of Trivial Pursuit |
| Cleanliness[4] | The smell of a citrus-scented all-purpose cleaner | People kept their desks significantly cleaner after eating food |
| Guilt[5] | Exposure to words about guilt (e.g., *guilty, remorse, sin*) | People were more likely to purchase candy (due to a "guilty pleasure") |

[1](Bargh, Chen, & Burrows, 1996) [2](Fitzsimons & Bargh, 2003) [3](Dijksterhuis & van Knippenberg, 1998) [4](Holland, Hendriks, & Aarts, 2005) [5](Goldsmith, Kim Cho, & Dhar, 2012)

Similar to the previous section, this section will describe some standard schemas that you can activate, along with a few other schemas that you can activate depending on the situation.

*Standard Schemas.* What's a good schema that can help you trigger compliance? You could use the same conversation-starter technique that was described in the previous section, except you could initiate a conversation revolving around compliance, rather than open-mindedness. A conversation about someone complying with a request might activate your target's schema for compliance, which could then trigger a certain behavior that your target associates with compliance—namely, compliance.

Another standard schema that has garnered support from research is helpfulness. When people were exposed to words relating to helpfulness, they were more likely to help an experimenter who accidentally dropped items after the experiment had supposedly ended (Macrae & Johnston, 1998). And as you can see from the list of priming studies, similar effects have been found for activating schemas of politeness (Bargh, Chen, & Burrows, 1996) and friendship (Fitzsimons & Bargh, 2003).

Finally, one last schema that you could activate in nearly any situation relates to a common social norm. Here's a hint: it involves an occasion that occurs once a year. Give up? For centuries, the idea of gift giving has become heavily associated with our schema for birthdays. As a result, if you prime someone's schema for birthday, you're likely to trigger behavior associated with gift giving.

If I wanted to make a viral video, I could put the odds in my favor by using that "birthday" technique to persuade a large group of my Facebook friends to initially share the video. How? Before posting the video to my Facebook and asking my friends to share it, I could change my profile picture to a picture of me cutting a cake on my birthday (no matter how far back in time the picture was taken). Exposing people to that picture would then prime their schema for birthdays, and subsequently, the idea of gift giving. Because the idea of gift giving would become activated upon that exposure, my Facebook friends would feel greater pressure to comply with a favor, such as to share my video. Could that simple technique really cause a video to go viral? I used that exact technique with my YouTube video, "Chat Roulette Mind Reading—Part 1," and an *astounding* number of my Facebook friends shared the video (which then went viral and reached almost a million views within the first week). There were obviously many other factors involved as well, but my new profile picture definitely didn't hurt.

You should also realize that these types of priming effects often occur outside of our conscious awareness. If people see the picture of me cutting my birthday cake, they don't need to think, "Oh, is it Nick's birthday? I should probably do something nice for him by sharing his video." In fact, they don't even need to consciously *notice* my new profile picture. Much like a subliminal exposure to Apple's logo can trigger creative behavior, a nonconscious exposure to my birthday-related picture can still trigger gift giving behavior. People will feel greater pressure to share my video, yet they won't know why. Oh, the beauty of priming.

*Other Schemas.* Suppose that you're a teacher with rowdy students, and you wanted to extract better behavior from them. What could you do?

One idea is to take advantage of another social norm: being silent in a library. When people in one experiment were primed with a picture of a library and were told that they would be visiting a library, not only did they identify words relating to silence (e.g., *silent, quiet, still, whisper*) more quickly, but they also demonstrated behavior consistent with the social norm of being in a library. Compared to people who were primed with a picture of a train station, people who were exposed to pictures of a library spoke using a quieter voice (Aarts & Dijksterhuis, 2003).

To extract better behavior from your students, you could do something similar. By hanging pictures of a library on the wall of your classroom, you can prime your students' schema for the library, which might activate behavior consistent with being in a library (i.e., being quiet). Although kids can be very difficult to persuade, if you use this strategy along with the other techniques in this book, you could start to regain control over your classroom.

The applications of priming are only limited by your imagination. Whenever you're trying to persuade someone to accept a message or comply with a request, always brainstorm a possible schema that you can activate to put the odds further in your favor. That simple technique could be the extra push that you need to secure your target's compliance.

## A MIND READER'S PERSPECTIVE: HOW TO READ MINDS USING PRIMING

I started performing magic shows at a very young age, but I always hated referring to myself as a magician. A "magician" always seems to bring up the image of a dorky guy in a tuxedo pulling a rabbit out of a hat, and that type of image didn't appeal to me (though I *am* a somewhat dorky guy, I don't own a tuxedo and I'm allergic to rabbits).

Even though I now perform as a "mind reader," nothing that I perform is based on any sort of supernatural phenomenon. In fact, there are only three main ways that anyone can "read minds." You can either:

1. Use magic and deception (e.g., sleight of hand) to make it seem like you knew what someone was thinking.
2. Rely on body language, nonverbal behavior, and other deductive cues to guess what someone is thinking.
3. Prime someone to think of a specific thought without their awareness and then proceed to "read their mind."

Which method do I use? I rely mostly on the third method, but I use the first and second methods to further enhance the impossibility of my demonstrations.

When I use the third method to nonconsciously influence people to think of something—whether it's the Easter Bunny, the color orange, or a dessert cake—I use subtle cues in my script to prime a particular thought. I described the demonstration with the number seven at the beginning of the chapter, but I'll give you another example. And again, go with the first answer that pops into your head. Think of a vegetable that you might find in a garden.

Are you thinking of a vegetable? Even though I was in the midst of describing how I use subtle cues to prime a specific thought, I was actually using subtle cues to prime the thought of a carrot. If you read back through this section, you'll notice that I make specific references to things that people associate with carrots—rabbits, the Easter Bunny, the color orange, a dessert cake (carrot cake). Consistent with spreading activation, those references would make your schema for "carrot" more readily available on a nonconscious level, and when you're forced to think quickly, your brain is more likely to choose a carrot because of that heightened activation. It's a pretty cool phenomenon.

# CHAPTER 2

# Anchor Their Perception

Once you mentally answer these next questions, think of your *exact* estimate for each question:

- ➤ Is the average temperature in San Francisco greater or less than 558 degrees Fahrenheit?
- ➤ Was the number of Beatles records that made the top ten greater or fewer than 100,025 records?
- ➤ Is the average price of a college textbook greater or less than $7,128.53?

Did you think of your exact estimates for each question? Let me guess. All of your exact estimates were far below the suggested numbers, right? No shocker there. The real shocker is that, despite those absurd numbers, they still likely influenced your final estimate to be higher than it would have been if those anchors weren't present (Quattrone et al., 1984). If you're skeptical, try it on your friends; ask some people those same three questions but without the anchors. There's a good chance that their estimate will be lower than your estimate.

That psychological principle—the *anchoring effect*—was popularized by Amos Tversky and Daniel Kahneman, two prolific researchers in human judgment and decision making (Tversky & Kahneman, 1974). They found that people tend to make judgments by using relative distances from anchor points.

The numeric anchors in the previous questions were essentially a type of prime because they each activated a certain mental image that influenced your estimates. Those suggested numbers primed you to think of a very hot day in San Francisco, a band with many records making the top ten, and a very expensive college textbook. With those mental images activated, you were more likely to make an estimate that was consistent with those mental images.

In addition to priming, however, there's another explanation behind that phenomenon. The anchoring effect is often referred to as the *anchoring and adjustment heuristic* because we often adjust our judgments in relation to some anchor point. For example, when you estimated the temperature in San Francisco after receiving an anchor point of 558 degrees Fahrenheit, you may have started from 558 degrees and adjusted your estimate downward until you reached an estimate that was more reasonable.

As you'll learn in this chapter, these adjustments (and the anchoring effect in general) can lead to some very inaccurate and potentially harmful judgments.

## THE POWER OF ANCHORS

Now that you've read the first chapter of this book, you now have a better idea about the quality of the content. Given what you know at this moment, how likely are you to purchase my next book? Is the probability greater or less than 90 percent? Now, make an *exact* estimate of how likely you are to purchase my next book.

Do you have your estimate? Whether or not you consciously realized it, you likely started at 90 percent and then adjusted your estimate upward or downward accordingly. In either case, however, your estimate is now higher than if I had asked you whether the probability was greater or less than 10 percent, a much lower anchor point.

But wait. When you estimated that probability, you already possessed a general understanding of anchoring because I described it at the beginning of the chapter. Wouldn't that knowledge help you produce a lower estimate to compensate for the 90 percent anchor that I gave? Ah, you'd think so, but unfortunately, anchoring is so powerful that we succumb to it even when we recognize its influence.

Perhaps the most striking finding from research is that even deliberate warnings about anchoring go unheeded. In one study, Wilson and colleagues (1996) asked people to estimate the number of physicians they believed would appear in a phone book, and they asked people to give their estimate after writing down a four-digit ID number. The researchers wanted to examine whether a deliberate warning about anchoring would affect their estimation, and so they warned people how their arbitrary ID number could influence their estimations:

> A number in people's heads can influence their answers to subsequent questions . . . When you answer the questions on the following pages, *please be careful not to have this contamination effect happen to you.* We would like the most accurate estimates that you can come up with. (Wilson et al., 1996, p. 397)

Surprisingly, despite that deliberate warning, people were still influenced by their arbitrary ID number when they estimated the number of physicians in the phone book. Even when people are fully aware of the powerful impact of anchoring, they still succumb to its influence. It doesn't get more powerful than that!

## WHY DO WE USE ANCHORS?

We already looked at two mechanisms that explain *how* anchoring can influence our judgments (i.e., through priming and adjustments), but this section will explain *why* we tend to rely on anchors to make judgments.

**Produce Accurate Judgments.** Perhaps the main reason why we use anchoring—either consciously or nonconsciously—is that we truly believe it leads to more accurate judgments. This section will discuss two pieces of evidence to support that notion: (1) people who are highly motivated to produce an accurate judgment still use anchoring, and (2) when no anchors are given, people often generate their own anchors to help make their judgment.

*Occurs When Motivation Is High.* The researchers who conducted the phone book experiment conducted another experiment where they gave people an incentive to produce accurate estimates. Participants in the experiment were told that the person with the closest estimate would receive a $50 prize, but the results showed that the incentive and additional motivation made no difference—the irrelevant ID number still influenced their estimates (Wilson et al., 1996).

Not only does anchoring influence trivial judgments, such as the number of physicians in a phonebook, but it can also influence very important decisions. Extensive research has applied the anchoring effect to criminal trials, and unfortunately, evidence shows that judges rely on anchors to determine the lengths of their sentencing. For instance, when legal professionals were asked to read a hypothetical shoplifting case and then decide a proper sentencing length, they were influenced by the prosecutor's recommended length, even when they were informed that the length was chosen at random:

> For experimental purposes, the following prosecutor's sentencing demand was randomly determined, therefore, it does not reflect any judicial expertise: The prosecutor demands a sentence [of] 3 months on probation. (Englich, Mussweiler, & Strack, 2006, p. 192)

When exposed to a 1 month demand from the defense and that 3 month demand from the prosecution, the legal experts gave an average sentence of 4 months. When the 3 months from the previous excerpt was replaced by 9 months, however, legal experts gave an average sentence of 6 months. The sentencing length increased by 2 months even though the description clearly mentioned that the suggested length was chosen at random.

A 2-month difference might not seem that substantial, but research has found differences in sentencing lengths that span several years (Pepitone & DiNubile, 1976), even when there is greater emphasis on the arbitrariness of the anchor, such as a recommended length that results from rolling a pair of dice (Englich, Mussweiler, & Strack, 2006). Therefore, even people with high expertise—such as legal professionals—use anchors to produce their judgments. It's truly mind-boggling how one quick exposure to an irrelevant number could change someone's life forever.

*We Use Self-Generated Anchors.* Further support for our misguided faith in anchors can be found in our tendency to use "self-generated anchors" (Epley & Gilovich, 2006). When we're facing a situation where no suitable anchor has been provided, we often seek our own anchor from which we can produce our judgment (hence the term, "self-generated anchor").

Suppose that you're applying for a job position and you're asked to input your desired salary (what an aggravating question, huh?). To produce your estimate, you would likely use a three-step anchoring process:

1. Determine the average salary for that type of position (perhaps through personal experience or a quick Google search).
2. Judge the reputation of the hiring company (whether the company seems above or below average).
3. Mentally start from the average salary and adjust your desired salary according to the reputation of the hiring company. If the company is very prestigious and reputable, you would likely adjust your desired salary upward from the average (and vice versa).

In that scenario, the average salary is considered a "self-generated anchor" because you created that anchor to produce your desired salary.

Self-generated anchors are used in many different circumstances, not just desired salaries. In one study, people were asked to give the freezing point of vodka—a question that most people were stumped to answer—and so they used the freezing point of water as an anchor point. People who realized that the freezing point of water was 0° Celsius realized that the freezing point of vodka must be lower, and they adjusted their estimate according to that anchor (Epley & Gilovich, 2006).

Although anchoring *can* lead to more accurate judgments (such as people who used the freezing point of water as an anchor point), it usually leads to poor judgments when we rely on the second reason behind our use of anchors: when we use anchors to exert less mental effort.

**Exert Less Mental Effort.** By nature, humans are lazy. Though we're motivated to produce accurate judgments, we often try to produce those judgments using the least amount of effort possible. Unfortunately, when we use anchors as a shortcut for our decision making, we usually fail to achieve our primary goal of forming an accurate judgment.

The following are two specific types of anchoring shortcuts that we sometimes use (and which often lead to poor judgments).

*Plausible Outcome Reached.* Remember when I asked you to estimate the probability of purchasing my next book? With such a hazy question, estimating your exact probability would have been fairly difficult. Rather than pull a number from thin air, you likely generated a *range* of reasonable probabilities.

Let's assume that you generated a range of 50–70 percent (which could have been produced either consciously or nonconsciously). If the initial anchor point was 90 percent, you would have determined your exact probability by adjusting downward from 90 percent until you reached the first plausible estimate in your range—in this case, it would have been 70 percent (the very top of your range of probabilities). On the flip side, if the initial anchor point was 10 percent, you would have determined your estimate by adjusting upward from

10 percent until you reached the first probability within your range—in this case, it would have been 50 percent (the very bottom of your range of probabilities). The takeaway: anchoring can produce inaccurate judgments because we often adjust from an anchor point until we reach the outermost estimate within a range of plausible judgments (Epley & Gilovich, 2006).

Applying that principle to courtrooms, suppose that the average sentencing length for a particular crime ranges from 2 to 4 years. If the prosecutor demands a sentence of 5 years, then the judge is likely to start from 5 years and adjust his sentence downward until he reaches the outermost sentence of 4 years. If the defense demands a sentence of 1 year, then the judge is likely to start from 1 year and adjust his sentence upward until he reaches the outermost sentence of 2 years. In either case, the difference is 2 years—a full 2 years of someone's life would be completely dependent on an arbitrary number presented to the judge.

*Availability Heuristic.* Another poor use of anchoring can be found in the *availability heuristic,* the tendency to evaluate the probability of an event by how easily an instance comes to our mind. When we receive an anchor, we might reflect on instances where that anchor is true, and if an instance comes to our mind very easily, then we might falsely assume that the anchor is accurate, and so we produce a judgment near that anchor point (Mussweiler & Strack, 2000).

In courtrooms, judges can falsely associate the ease with which a particular sentence length comes to mind with the frequency of that sentencing. If a prosecutor demands 5 years for a crime, the judge may reflect on past cases where that same sentence was given for that crime. If he can easily think of a particular instance, then he might assume that the length of his sentence should also fall near that anchor of 5 years.

What makes this application of anchoring particularly unfortunate is that there are many reasons why a particular sentence would come to the judge's mind besides the frequency of that sentence. Perhaps a 5-year sentence for a particular crime popped into his mind more easily not because of its frequency but because the criminal's actions in that case were particularly atrocious and memorable. In this scenario, the 5-year sentence would be longer than the average length for that crime, but the judge would falsely believe that it's an average length. Due to this unfortunate circumstance, people who commit a minor crime might receive a much longer sentence than they deserve because of that mistaken judgment.

## WHAT DETERMINES THE DIRECTION OF ADJUSTMENT?

This chapter has mainly focused on *assimilation*: judgments have mostly adjusted *toward* a provided anchor. However, anchoring can also produce *contrast effects*: judgments can also adjust *away* from a provided anchor. To experience a contrast effect, look at the following optical illusion, known as the Ebbinghaus illusion:

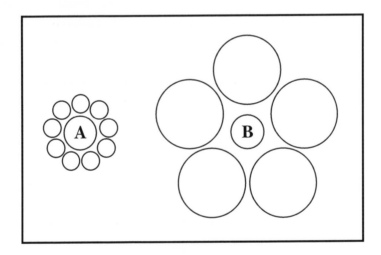

Which circle is larger: A or B? Circle A is larger, right? It seems that way, but both circles are actually the same size. This optical illusion demonstrates a *contrast effect*, the tendency to perceive a stimulus differently depending on the surrounding stimuli. When you judged the size of A and B, your perception was anchored by the surrounding circles: the smaller circles around Circle A caused you to perceive a larger relative size, whereas the larger circles surrounding Circle B caused you to perceive a smaller relative size. This difference in perception is often referred to as *perceptual contrast.*

Contrast effects influence our perception not only with arbitrary circles but with many different types of stimuli each day, including our perception of other people's attractiveness. For example, researchers showed men a picture of a female after the men had watched *Charlie's Angels*—a television show from the 1970s with three very attractive females as the main characters. Compared to a control group, men who had been watching *Charlie's Angels* rated the female in the picture to be less attractive because the television show created a contrast effect (Kenrick & Gutierres, 1989).

Like assimilation, contrast effects alter our perception on a daily basis without our awareness. For example, these effects can influence whether you choose to eat an unhealthy meal or an organic fruit salad. To demonstrate, estimate the calorie content in a typical cheeseburger. Keep that exact estimate in the back of your mind because we'll return to it in a second.

But now that you understand the difference between assimilation (adjusting *toward* anchors) and contrast effects (adjusting *away from* anchors), what determines those directions? When do we adjust toward an anchor, and when do we adjust away from an anchor? One main factor involves the extremity of an anchor. When someone is forming a judgment, an anchor that is very extreme will trigger a contrast effect.

Do you recall your estimate of the calorie content in a typical cheeseburger? If you were to ask other people that same question, their estimate would likely be lower than yours. Why? Immediately before I asked you to estimate, I subtly mentioned an organic fruit salad. Although you might not have realized it, that cue became an extreme anchor point that influenced you to perceive a cheeseburger as having more calories.

A recent study confirmed that same outcome (Chernev, 2011). People who were primed to think of "an organic fruit salad" (an anchor point that's positioned on the extreme *low* end of the calorie spectrum) adjusted their calorie estimate of a subsequent cheeseburger *away* from the low end because that extreme anchor point made the calorie difference seem more pronounced. In a sense, the very healthy fruit salad became one of the smaller surrounding circles in the optical illusion, which caused you to perceive a large number of calories in a cheeseburger. Conversely, people who were primed to think of a "decadent cheesecake" (an anchor point that's positioned on the extreme *high* end of the calorie spectrum) adjusted their calorie estimate of a cheeseburger *away* from the high end. The cheeseburger became the seemingly smaller Circle B because the very unhealthy cheesecake made the number of calories in a cheeseburger seem fewer.

This chapter described how assimilation toward an arbitrary prison sentence length can alter a person's life, and unfortunately, contrast effects are no different. When judges evaluate a homicide case (an anchor that lies on the egregious end of the crime spectrum), they tend to perceive subsequent cases to be less severe. If an assault case is presented immediately following a homicide case, the judge tends to issue sentences that are shorter than the average length for assaults because of perceptual contrast. Likewise, a homicide that is judged after an assault case is perceived to be more severe, and the judge tends to issue a sentence that is longer than average (Pepitone & DiNubile, 1976).

Before continuing, you should realize that contrast effects occur only with semantic categories (e.g., types of food, types of crime). The good news is that nearly all numeric anchors cause assimilation. Much like how people give higher estimates of Gandhi's age when they're asked if he was younger or older than 140 (Strack & Mussweiler, 1997), *any* number that you present to your target—whether that number is relevant, arbitrary, or absurdly extreme—will cause people to adjust their judgment *toward* that number.

# PERSUASION STRATEGY: ANCHOR THEIR PERCEPTION

There are plenty of instances where providing an anchor could boost your persuasion. Perhaps you're a salesperson sending an e-mail to customers asking if they want to reorder your products; why not offer a numeric anchor that's higher than average? That higher number would become an anchor point that your customers would assimilate toward, leading to a larger purchase than they would typically buy.

But besides those basic anchoring strategies, there are many other persuasion applications that aren't so obvious. This section will explain some clever strategies to give you an idea of the sheer potential of anchoring.

**Present a Decoy.** As Dan Ariely (2009) describes in *Predictably Irrational*, the options that you present to your target can become anchor points that people use to compare the other options. Imagine that you're deciding between two subscriptions to a magazine:

➤ **Product A:** Online subscription for $59.
➤ **Product B:** Online *and* print subscription for $125.

When presented with those options, 68 percent of students chose the online subscription and 32 percent chose the online and print subscription, a distribution that resulted in $8,012 of revenue.

But something fascinating happened when a new subscription option was added. Take a look at the product marked as "B–" (to imply that the product is similar to Product B, yet worse in one aspect):

➤ **Product A:** Online subscription for $59.
➤ **Product B–:** Print subscription for $125.
➤ **Product B:** Online *and* print subscription for $125.

If you present those options to people, you'd be hard-pressed to find even one person who would choose Product B–. Why would you choose a print only subscription when you could choose the online *and* print for the same price?

And your intuitive judgment would be correct; when that new option was given to a sample of students, not one person chose it. Nevertheless, its mere presence drastically changed the outcome and increased revenue from $8,012 to $11,444. Why? The percentage of people choosing the online only subscription dropped from 68 percent to 16 percent, whereas the percentage of people choosing the online and print subscription (a more expensive option) increased from 32 percent to 84 percent.

Due to contrast effects, Product B became a seemingly better option because people could compare it to Product B–, a clearly worse option. Because there was no equivalent product to which Product A could be compared, people were more likely to choose Product B because they perceived it to be the best option.

When people are undecided between two different options, you can influence them to choose a particular option by adding a new option that is similar to one, but either better or worse in some aspect. When you add that similar option into the mix, you give people an anchor that they can use to judge the existing similar option. If the new option is better, then the new option is perceived as the clear winner, but if the new option is worse, then the already existing similar option becomes the clear winner.

To apply this "decoy effect" toward your business, suppose that you're selling consulting services. It might be favorable for you to offer three options: one option that is priced low, one option that is priced moderately, and one option that is priced extremely high. The very high priced option will convert more people from the low priced option to the moderately priced option, helping to generate more overall revenue for your business (Huber, Payne, & Puto, 1982).

Even if you're not selling products, you could apply the decoy effect toward minuscule life moments, such as influencing your friends to eat at a particular restaurant. Suppose that you're arguing with your friends about where to eat. Some are arguing for a particular Mexican restaurant, whereas you and a few others are pulling for a particular

Chinese restaurant. If you know that your friends dislike another particular Chinese restaurant, you could put the odds in your favor by throwing that option into the mix Because that option is similar to yours but worse in some respect, you trigger a contrast effect that will make your existing Chinese restaurant seem even better.

**Door-in-the-Face Technique.** To help spread the word about my book to other people, would you mind purchasing additional copies to give to your friends or coworkers? What? You don't want to do that? Alright, well, would you mind just purchasing a copy of my next book for yourself?

The previous paragraph illustrates the *door-in-the-face technique*, the strategy of asking for a very large request and then following with a much smaller request. A large favor can trigger a contrast effect that can make another favor seem even smaller, which can help you garner higher rates of compliance with that separate request.

In the original study that examined this technique, Robert Cialdini and his colleagues (1975) asked random college students to volunteer at a juvenile delinquency center for two hours each week over the next two years. You can probably guess what happened. Everyone immediately jumped at the incredible opportunity, right? Not quite. As expected, nearly everyone politely turned down that large request.

But something interesting happened when the researchers followed that large request with a smaller request: to take the juvenile delinquents on a two-hour trip to the zoo. Without that initial large request, only 17 percent of people agreed to the zoo trip, but when that initial large request *was* presented (and rejected), compliance for the zoo trip request nearly tripled to 50 percent. The large request created an anchor from which people could judge the size of the zoo trip. With such a large anchor established, the zoo trip was perceived to be much smaller, thereby leading to a higher rate of compliance.

**Convey High Expectations.** Although I might be biased, I truly believe that this book is very informative, helpful, and interesting. I'd even go so far as to say that you'll rate it a 10 out of 10.

The two previous strategies in this chapter (i.e., presenting a decoy and the door-in-the-face technique) involved contrast effects; there wasn't any "assimilation" toward an anchor point. However, one strategy that *does* involve our tendency to adjust our judgment *toward* an anchor point involves conveying the appropriate expectations, such as the suggestion that you'll rate this book a 10 out of 10.

How can you apply this strategy in your own life? Suppose that you're submitting an essay to your professor, and your professor asks you how you think it turned out. What would you say? To secure the highest grade possible, you could take advantage of anchoring by making a joke that you think your paper is "worthy of an A." On the surface, it seems like an innocent remark. But as the devious persuasion mastermind you are, you realize that mentioning an "A" establishes an anchor point that your professor will use when grading your paper. With his perception anchored toward the high end of the grading scale, his grade will likely be higher than if he didn't receive that anchor point. If legal experts with thirty years of experience are influenced by anchoring, there's no reason why professors would be any different.

Conveying high expectations can be an extremely powerful persuasion tool for many reasons. This strategy is so powerful that I devoted the next chapter to it.

## A MIND READER'S PERSPECTIVE:
## HOW I USE ANCHORING IN A $100 DEMONSTRATION

In the opening demonstration of my mind reading show, I play a game where one of three volunteers can win one hundred dollars (and unbeknownst to the audience, I use anchoring to put the odds in my favor).

Hanging from my table are four envelopes (each are labeled "1", "2", "3", and "4", respectively), and I explain that one of those envelopes contains a one hundred dollar bill. I bring three volunteers on stage and ask each of them to choose an envelope, and I explain that if they choose the envelope with the money, then they can keep it. When I ask the first volunteer to choose an envelope, I say:

*I've performed this demonstration many times on stage. And for the last five times that I've performed it, the money has been in envelope number three. Now why am I telling you that? Am I trying to influence you to pick envelope number three, or am I trying to use reverse psychology to try to nudge you toward a different envelope?*

Except for a few very rare cases, the volunteer in this scenario usually chooses the second envelope. Why? Ask a friend to think of a number between one and four. Chances are high that the person will choose two or three (with the number three being chosen more often). People very rarely choose one or four because they stick out too much (and not to mention that you subtly imply that they should choose a number "between" one and four).

But why do volunteers choose envelope two, and not envelope three? If you notice, my scripting discourages people from choosing the third envelope because I bring the volunteer's attention to it. By outwardly mentioning that the money has frequently been in the third envelope, people no longer feel comfortable selecting it; if they choose the third envelope, they'll appear gullible in the eyes of the audience (a perception that they try to avoid). Because people still feel compelled to choose an option from the middle, they pick the only remaining option in the middle: envelope number two.

After the first volunteer chooses the second envelope, I proceed to the next volunteer. Because the first volunteer didn't select the third envelope (despite my claim that the money has frequently been in that envelope), this second volunteer now feels greater pressure to select the third envelope. If he doesn't select it, then the third volunteer may not select it either. If I ended up with the money from envelope number three, then all of the volunteers would seem stupid, a perception that the second volunteer avoids by selecting envelope number three.

At this point, I've eliminated envelopes two and three from the equation, and now I just need to influence the third volunteer's choice of envelope. In fact, I've already subtly influenced him to choose envelope number four. Can you think of why? Here's a hint: it has to do with anchoring.

In the excerpt from my script, I mentioned that the money has been in the third envelope for the last "five" demonstrations (and I consistently remind the audience of that). Therefore, the last volunteer is more likely to choose envelope number four because I set a nonconscious anchor that was higher than the two remaining choices. When the final volunteer must choose between one and four, she is likely to start at the anchor of "five" and adjust downward until she reaches the first plausible choice (i.e., envelope four).

Feel free to try this demonstration with your friends but do *not* try this demonstration with real money. Psychological tactics are never foolproof, and so I always have multiple backup plans in my demonstrations in case the psychology doesn't pan out the way it should (which can often happen).

# CHAPTER 3

# Convey High Expectations

You're walking through a subway station, and you walk past a violinist. You casually listen to him as you walk by, but you continue toward your destination without skipping a beat. Nothing really fazes you.

Now fast forward two weeks. Your friend just gave you a generous birthday gift: two expensive tickets to a world famous violinist. Although you've never heard of him, you're very excited to witness one of the greatest musicians in the world.

The night of the concert finally arrives, and you're seated in the theater, anxiously waiting for the performance to start. The violinist steps on to the stage, and the concert begins. As soon as he starts playing, you're blown away. You've never been exposed to a quality violin performance, and so you're truly captivated by the musician's talent. By the end of the night, you're brought to tears, and you give him a standing ovation for one of the best performances that you've ever witnessed.

Quiz time . . . What was the difference between the first violinist in the subway station and the violinist at the concert? The musician in the subway station was only half-decent, and the musician at the concert was among the best in the world, right? What if the world famous violinist was the same person who was playing in the subway station? Surely, you still would have noticed the beauty and talent of his performance, right?

On January 12 of 2007, a violinist played for 45 minutes in the L'Enfant Plaza subway station in Washington DC. During those 45 minutes, a few people stopped to donate a couple dollars, but nothing happened that was out of the ordinary. Nearly everyone walked by at their usual pace without stopping to listen or pay attention. Why is that surprising? The violinist, Joshua Bell, is one of the greatest violinists in the world. Two days prior to his performance in the subway station, Bell performed at a sold-out theater in Boston where tickets cost roughly $100 per seat. It was reported that he even purchased his violin at a staggering price of $3.5 million. Needless to say, Bell is considered one of the greatest musicians in the world.

Why were people unfazed by his performance in the subway station? Why did most people simply walk by without stopping to listen to his incredible music? Is it really possible for someone to be blown away by Bell's performance at a theater yet remain completely unfazed by him in a subway station? After reading this chapter, you'll understand why that outcome is very possible. The explanation behind that surprising phenomenon relates to our expectations and how they mold our perception of the world.

## THE POWER OF EXPECTATIONS

Similar to mindsets, our expectations largely dictate our perception of the world. Whenever we develop expectations for a certain event, our brain often molds our perception of that event to match our expectations. We see what we expect to see. We hear what we expect to hear. We feel what we expect to feel.

Placebo effects are a clear example of that concept. When researchers test a new drug on patients, they give some people the actual drug, and they give other people a fake version of the drug (i.e., a placebo) that produces no effect. This procedure is needed because our expectations can often dictate the outcome of treatments. We usually show signs of improvement after receiving a placebo merely because we *expect* to show signs of improvement.

Although placebo effects are typically associated with testing new antibiotics, your expectations influence you every day. Do you prefer Coke or Pepsi? Recent research has revealed some interesting findings in that choice. Because Coke is the dominant brand, most people have developed the expectation that Coke tastes better, and research confirms that people *do* prefer Coke over Pepsi in non-blind taste tests (i.e., when people know which drink they're consuming). But an interesting phenomenon occurs when the taste tests are blind. When people aren't told which drink they're consuming—an event that eliminates expectations from the equation—more people prefer the taste of Pepsi (McClure et al., 2004).

Perhaps even more interesting is that this "Pepsi Paradox" is completely eliminated for people with damage to their ventromedial prefrontal cortex, an area of the brain associated with emotion. People with this brain damage prefer the taste of Pepsi, even when they know which drink they're consuming, because they're not susceptible to the emotional expectations stemming from the popularity of Coke (Koenigs & Tranel, 2008).

When our brains are healthy, high expectations can lead to more neural activity in the brain region associated with pleasantness. A group of researchers studied neural activity in people when they drank wine that was marked at various price points, and even though they used the same wine in each condition, the wine that was marked at higher price points had sparked more neural activity in the orbitofrontal cortex, the brain region associated with pleasantness (Plassman et al., 2008). People found the taste of wine more pleasing when they *merely believed* it was purchased at a higher price. Therefore, expectations are very powerful because they can mold our perception, even from a biological perspective.

Not only can expectations mold our perception, but they can also influence our behavior. In another experiment, some people purchased an energy drink at a full price of $1.89, whereas other people purchased the same energy drink at a discount price of $0.89. The researchers wanted to examine whether people's knowledge of the drink's price would influence their performance on a mental task, and the results were pretty enlightening. People who purchased the drink at full price performed significantly better than people who purchased the drink at a discount, even though the drink was exactly the same in each condition (Shiv, Carmon, & Ariely, 2005). People who purchased the drink at full price developed higher expectations for the drink's effectiveness, thereby causing them to perform better on the mental task, whereas people who purchased the drink at a discount developed lower expectations, causing them to perform worse on the mental task. Even something as innocent as the price of an energy drink can convey certain expectations, which can then influence our perception and behavior.

## WHY ARE EXPECTATIONS SO POWERFUL?

Why are expectations so powerful? One potential explanation lies in anchoring. Much like we adjust from an anchor point toward a *range* of plausible estimations (e.g., a 50–70 percent likelihood of purchasing my next book), we also seem to adjust toward a range of plausible expectations. For example, when you purchased this book, it would be impossible to know exactly how good it would be, so you likely developed a range of expectations.

Now, suppose that before you read this book, your friend told you that it was the best book that he's ever read, thereby setting an anchor point on the high end of an expectation spectrum. When you actually read the book, you might adjust downward from that anchor point until you reach the outermost point of your original range, which would naturally be near the high end. On the other hand, if you received an anchor point that was lower than your range, you may adjust upward from that anchor until you reach the outermost bottom of that range. In either case, your expectations—high or low—acted like an anchor point that molded your perception.

Similarly, because extreme anchors can produce contrast effects, expectations can also backfire if they're too extreme. If your friend mentioned that this book was so good that it could spur a new religion or bring about the destruction of the entire world, then those expectations would likely produce a contrast effect and worsen your actual opinion of the book.

Nonetheless, research shows that conveying high (yet believable) expectations will usually lead someone to perceive an event to match those expectations. In addition to an anchoring mechanism, there are a few other principles that can explain why expectations are so powerful in certain situations.

**Confirmation Bias.** First, our expectations can mold our perception because of *confirmation bias*, which is the natural tendency for people to seek information to confirm their beliefs or expectations (Nickerson, 1998).

Suppose that you believe in aliens, yet you're trying to make an unbiased decision regarding whether or not they actually exist. If you wanted to research the subject more thoroughly, you might turn to Google and search "videos of aliens." Whoops. You've already fallen prey to confirmation bias because those search terms subtly acknowledge their existence. Most of the results that appear will be sources that support their existence, thereby leading you to a biased conclusion that they *do* exist.

We feel a strong desire to confirm our expectations because it feels upsetting when information disconfirms our expectations. Like most people, you probably cringe whenever you hear a recording of your own voice. The voice projecting from that device sounds so foreign that it can't possibly be your voice. But wait. Is your distaste resulting from a poor recording device or is your distaste resulting from your expectations?

When we speak, our brain hears a voice that's different from the voice that other people hear. When we project our voice, the muscles that produce our speech cause a vibration that runs from our neck to our brain's auditory mechanisms, and those vibrations internally distort our voice. Because those vibrations occur internally, other people (including voice recorders) hear your voice without those distortions—i.e., your true external voice. Over time, you become so familiar with your internally distorted voice that when you hear your true voice from a recorder, your voice sounds very different, and those incongruent expectations are the culprit behind your distaste toward the sound of your voice. The best way to develop an appreciation for your voice is to become accustomed to the way it truly sounds. People with a background in voice work (e.g., radio hosts) eventually grow to enjoy the sound of their voice because the frequent exposure helps them develop the appropriate expectations.

How do we overcome incongruent expectations in other situations? One popular technique is *selective avoidance*: we simply ignore information that disconfirms our expectations. Oftentimes, our brains can be a mystery. In fact, read the following statement:

**OUR**

**BRAINS**

**CAN BE A**

**A MYSTERY**

Read that statement again. Notice anything unusual? Chances are high that you missed the extra "A" before "MYSTERY."

After I mentioned that "our brains can be a mystery" and asked you to read that additional statement, you encountered similar wording and probably expected that blurb to be the same as my original statement. Your expectations likely molded your perception of that blurb and caused you to skim over that discrepancy so that you could confirm your expectations. But now that your conscious mind is aware of that extra word, that discrepancy becomes so obvious that it can be amazing how you could have missed such a glaring error in the first place.

**Self-Fulfilling Prophecies.** In all of the previous explanations—anchoring, confirmation bias, and selective avoidance—the objective reality of an event never changed. The only thing that changed was our interpretation. However, our expectations can also change the objective reality.

Suppose that your friend Debbie is introducing you to her friend Emily. Before you meet Emily, Debbie describes her as cold, standoff-ish, and unfriendly, which causes you to develop the expectation that you won't get along with her. And upon meeting Emily, you find that your expectation is met: her personality seems very distant and unapproachable, and you can't seem to connect with her. When the conversation ends, you leave with no future intention of interacting with Emily again because of her unfriendly demeanor.

But let's backtrack for a second. Rather than Debbie describing Emily as cold and unapproachable, suppose that she described her as friendly, kind, and light-hearted. This description would cause you to develop a completely different set of expectations about Emily's personality. Upon meeting her with those new expectations, you instead find that her personality is very warm, fun, and energetic. When the conversation ends, you leave with high hopes of interacting with her again.

Assuming that Emily was the same person in each scenario, were those outcomes due to your perception of Emily, or were they due to Emily's actual behavior toward you? Trick question. Both your perception *and* Emily's actual behavior changed because of your expectations.

Remember the opening anecdote with the violinist? In that situation, only your perception was influenced. You weren't interacting with the violinist, so your expectations didn't influence him or his musical abilities in any way. His musical abilities in the subway station and at the expensive concert were exactly the same; the difference in your perception occurred solely through your interpretation.

In the situation with Emily, however, you *did* interact with her, and so you *were* able to influence her reaction and behavior toward you. More importantly, your initial behavior toward Emily largely resulted from your expectations. When Debbie described her as cold and unapproachable, your expectations of Emily's unfriendly attitude caused you to act in a negative fashion toward her. If Emily was an unfriendly person, why should you make an effort to extend a positive attitude toward her? Thus, it was *you*, not Emily, who became the first person to exude an unfriendly demeanor. As a result of *your* negative attitude, Emily reacted in a similar negative fashion (a typical response of any normal human being). When Emily matched your unfriendly demeanor, you misinterpreted that behavior as emerging solely from her. From your perspective, you were acting like your normal self, and it was Emily who was acting unfriendly.

On the flip side, when you discovered that Emily's personality was fun and lighthearted, you were excited to meet her. When conversing with Emily, your personality was upbeat and energetic because you expected that you would get along with her. As a result of *your* friendly demeanor, Emily then acted in a similar fashion and extended a positive attitude toward you.

The previous illustration can be explained by a *self-fulfilling prophecy* (Rist, 1970). Our expectations for an event are often met because they can cause us to behave in ways that lead to the expected outcome, such as in the previous illustration with Emily. Even if your expectations are false or inaccurate, those expectations can alter your behavior in a way that will cause the expected outcome to occur, hence the term "self-fulfilling prophecy."

We're usually guided by self-fulfilling prophecies every day without realizing it. Imagine that you're studying for an exam. If you expect to perform poorly, you might trigger a self-fulfilling prophecy and fail the exam because you'll engage in behaviors to fulfill your expectations (e.g., not studying). Why would you bother studying if you're just going to fail anyway? Studying would be useless. However, if you expect to perform well on the exam, you'll be more likely to engage in behavior to fulfill those hopeful expectations, namely by studying more and doing the proper things to help you pass the exam (e.g., eating well, getting enough sleep, etc.).

Hopefully my high expectations for this book have helped me write a book that you find interesting and informative. While writing this book, I developed the expectation that this book was going to be great, and though I can't be the one to judge, I *can* tell you that I've been spending nearly 15 hours every day for the past few months slaving over this book. My expectations were so high that I even quit my consulting job to finish writing it, and I've been surviving on a ramen noodle diet for the past few months so that I could afford to finish it. If my expectations were low, I wouldn't be pushing myself to the brink of mental and physical exhaustion to write this book.

Why did I just reveal that to you? You should know the answer by now: to convey high expectations for this book, of course.

## PERSUASION STRATEGY: CONVEY HIGH EXPECTATIONS

If you want people to perceive something more favorably, you should convey high expectations because those expectations will become a lens that will mold their perception. Although that's a clear implication from this chapter, this section will explain another key facet of that strategy.

**First Impressions.** Quick. Take five seconds to estimate the value of the following equation:

$$1 \times 2 \times 3 \times 4 \times 5 \times 6 \times 7 \times 8$$

Now that you have your answer, do you think that your answer would have been different if instead I asked you to calculate the following equation:

$$8 \times 7 \times 6 \times 5 \times 4 \times 3 \times 2 \times 1$$

Both equations are essentially the same; the only difference is the order of the numbers. Because both equations produce the same results, it's safe to assume that your guess would have been the same, right? *Au contraire.* Research shows that your guess would have been very different if I asked you to estimate the second equation instead of the first.

Amos Tversky and Daniel Kahneman (1973) conducted that study and found that people who were shown the first equation estimated a median of 512, and people who were shown the second equation estimated a median of 2,250.

Logic and rationale suggest that people's answers should have been the same, so what sparked that difference? The answer can be found in the *primacy effect,* which describes how information presented earlier in a sequence can produce a greater impact than information presented later in a sequence (Murdock, 1962). You can think of the primacy effect as a type of anchor. Those initial numbers set a specific anchor (either high or low depending on the equation), which influenced people's estimates.

To understand how that relates to expectations, consider an experiment where two groups of people were told that they would soon interact with another person. The first group learned that this person was "intelligent, industrious, impulsive, critical, stubborn, and envious," whereas the second group received that same information in the reverse order (i.e., "envious, stubborn, critical, impulsive, industrious, and intelligent"). Therefore, both groups received the same information, except the first group received the information with positive traits appearing first, and the second group received the information with negative traits appearing first.

Now that you understand the primacy effect, you can probably guess what happened. The group that was exposed to the initial positive traits had developed a much more favorable impression of the person with whom they interacted (Asch, 1946). Those initial traits molded participants' expectations for the remainder of the information in that sequence. Once they formed that initial impression, they devoted less attention to the remainder of the sequence because they assumed that their initial impression was accurate enough.

What's the practical takeaway? First impressions are absolutely critical. People's initial exposure to your message will mold their perception for the remainder of your message. In order to maximize your persuasion, you need to create a strong initial impression so that you convey high expectations for the rest of your message. As you'll learn in Chapter 11, this principle applies whenever you sequence multiple forms of justification, such as supporting arguments in a school essay or business proposal.

## A HYPNOTIST'S PERSPECTIVE:
## WHY HIGH EXPECTATIONS CAN MAKE
## SOMEONE A SUPERB HYPNOSIS SUBJECT

In addition to possessing a strong background as a mind reader, I also have a background in hypnosis. However, I choose not to perform hypnosis for entertainment because I don't want to tarnish people's perception of it. While hypnosis can be very entertaining, people often develop misconceptions about it because they only know it through the lens of entertainment. In reality, hypnosis is a very powerful clinical technique that can treat a wide range of conditions and habits (some common uses are smoking cessation and weight loss).

Nonetheless, one interesting facet about hypnosis is that expectations largely determine the extent that someone can be hypnotized. To understand that notion, you should first know that nearly every single person can be hypnotized. More importantly, research has found that there are very few distinct characteristics of people who *are* highly hypnotizable. In other words, the types of people that can easily be hypnotized can possess a wide range of personality traits; there is not *one* type of hypnotizable person.

Further, the few things that *do* determine if someone is hypnotizable can be controlled by the individual. For example, people are more likely to be hypnotized if they *expect* that they will by hypnotized or if they believe that they are the type of person who can easily be hypnotized (Gandhi & Oakley, 2005). Therefore, to successfully hypnotize someone, you need to convey the expectation that you *can* hypnotize them.

I still remember the first person that I ever tried to hypnotize. My friend desperately wanted to quit smoking, and I really wanted to help him. I had been studying hypnosis at the time, so I decided to put my knowledge to the first official test. Even though my inside thoughts were still somewhat skeptical of hypnosis (I honestly didn't think that it would work), I recognized that I should still convey the appropriate expectations.

Rather than outwardly state my skepticism, I projected a fake air of confidence to assure my friend that it would work. My friend witnessed my confidence and assurance in the hypnosis, and he then became more confident and assured in my ability to hypnotize him. As a result of his heightened expectations, I was able to guide him into a deep state of hypnosis, and after 10 minutes of giving him a few helpful suggestions toward his smoking habit, I guided him out of hypnosis, and he's been smoke-free to this day.

From that moment, I started conveying the same expectations for everyone else that I hypnotize, even to this day. If I'm hypnotizing someone that I just met, after 5 to 10 minutes of speaking with him, I smile and say, "It's funny. You seem like a very hypnotizable person. You seem like someone who could easily go into a deep state of hypnosis. That's a great quality to have." Because many people have doubts about their ability to be hypnotized (often because of how it's portrayed on stage), that statement removes any mental defenses that the person may possess, and it reinforces their expectations that they *will* be hypnotized. In turn, that makes it easier for me to guide them into a deep state of hypnosis.

Although I learned hypnosis mainly by studying the academic research on the subject, I recommend seeking proper training if you're interested in learning it. Hypnotherapy training is offered throughout the country and probably near your location. Hypnosis is a fantastic skill to possess, but because it can be very powerful, you should seek proper training if you're interested in learning it.

# REAL WORLD APPLICATION:
# THE FAMILY VACATION (PART 1)

At the end of each step in METHODS, I'll present a "Real World Application" to demonstrate how you can begin implementing that step into daily scenarios. In this first application, you want your family to take a vacation in a few months, but you expect to encounter some resistance from your budget-concerned husband. You know that your family has enough money saved, so you decide to implement a few tactics to make him more open-minded.

Considering your seven-year-old daughter, Mackenzie, you decide that a small trip to Disneyland would not only give her a great memory, but it would also be an affordable vacation compared to a worldwide alternative. In order to make your husband more open to that idea, you plan to anchor his perception by gathering travel information for two potential vacations: (1) a very expensive vacation around the world, and (2) the trip to Disneyland on which you have your heart set.

You know that your budget-concerned husband would never go for the first option, so you plan to present that decoy to set an absurdly high anchor point. When you present the second vacation option (the trip to Disneyland), a contrast effect will make this vacation seem much smaller because of your husband's newly anchored perception.

He gets home from work one day, and you put that plan into action. But before you bring up the idea about taking a family vacation, you put the odds further in your favor by mentioning that Mackenzie has been starting to eat vegetables—a food that she's always disliked. With this conversation involving Mackenzie's open-mindedness, you hope to activate your husband's schema for open-mindedness so that he will temporarily develop a more open-minded perception.

As you transition from that conversation into the idea about taking a vacation (e.g., "Speaking of Mackenzie . . ."), you present the very expensive vacation option, which he immediately rejects, as expected. But with his perception attached to that high anchor point, you then present the second option about the trip to Disneyland. With an intense look of contemplation, he mentions that he's on the fence and that he'll need time to think about it.

Darn. It wasn't the response that you wanted, but don't worry. This book will explain an enormous number of additional persuasion tactics that you can use to crack your husband's closed-mindedness. We'll revisit this scenario later, and I'll explain how you can incorporate other persuasion tactics to garner his compliance.

# STEP 2

# Elicit Congruent Attitudes

| | | | |
|---|---|---|---|
| **Before the Request** | *Step 1:* | **M** | Mold Their Perception |
| | ***Step 2:*** | **E** | **Elicit Congruent Attitudes** |
| | *Step 3:* | **T** | Trigger Social Pressure |
| | *Step 4:* | **H** | Habituate Your Message |
| **During the Request** | *Step 5:* | **O** | Optimize Your Message |
| | *Step 6:* | **D** | Drive Their Momentum |
| **After the Request** | *Step 7:* | **S** | Sustain Their Compliance |

## OVERVIEW:
## ELICIT CONGRUENT ATTITUDES

I mentioned in the introduction to this book that part of my goal was to make this book the most highlighted book in your collection. Though a seemingly innocent statement, it contained a few powerful psychological principles:

➤ First, that statement primed the idea of highlighting, which made you more likely to engage in that behavior (Chapter 1: Prime Their Mindset).

➤ The fact that I mentioned this book should be the most highlighted book in your collection conveyed high expectations (Chapter 3: Convey High Expectations). With your heightened expectations, you were likely to engage in a self-fulfilling prophecy by highlighting more than you typically would. Though that statement wouldn't have worked if you never highlight at all, I'm sure that there *are* many people reading this book that *are* highlighting more than they typically would.

But there's another very important benefit from mentioning that statement about highlighting, and this benefit is the main focus of the second step in METHODS:

➤ If you see yourself highlighting more than you typically would highlight, you're likely to develop a congruent attitude that this book is very helpful and informative.

The term "congruent" essentially means "consistent." If your target is engaging in a certain behavior (e.g., highlighting), he will feel greater pressure to develop an attitude that is "congruent" with his behavior. For example, if he's highlighting more than he would typically highlight, then he will infer that he must really like this book.

That notion is the main principle of Step 2 in METHODS. Because people experience a natural urge to hold attitudes that are consistent with their behavior, you can elicit an attitude that would be favorable for your situation by altering someone's body language or behavior to reflect that attitude. The next two chapters will explain why this principle is so powerful and how you can start applying it.

# CHAPTER 4

# Control Body Language

While you read this opening description of the chapter, place a pen in your mouth, and bite it with your teeth. Keep holding it with your teeth until you reach the next section . . . I'll explain why in a few paragraphs.

Body language is a booming topic. Walk into any bookstore and you're bound to find a large assortment of books about how you can use body language to instantly decode someone's inner thoughts. Unfortunately, many of those books are inaccurate and misleading because they make claims that are only based on intuition, rather than credible research. Does that mean the field of body language is doomed? Nope. Luckily, although some aspects make the field of body language seem like a pseudoscience, there *has* been some credible evidence to support some surprising claims. Accordingly, all of the principles in this chapter are grounded in that credible research.

Specifically, this chapter focuses on one fascinating topic that's been attracting a lot of attention from researchers over the past decade: *embodied cognition*. Embodied cognition can explain why:

➤ A job applicant has a better chance of getting the job if his résumé is attached to a heavy clipboard compared to a lighter clipboard (Jostmann, Lakens, & Schubert, 2009).
➤ Writing down negative thoughts about yourself can lower your self-esteem, but only when you write those thoughts with your dominant hand (Briñol & Petty, 2008).
➤ People who press their arm upward against a table eat significantly more cookies than people who press their arm downward on a table (Förster, 2003).

Embodied cognition asserts that the mind and body are intertwined. We typically assume that the mind influences the body, but the relationship also works in the reverse direction. That is, your body and behavioral actions can influence your thoughts, perception, attitudes, and many other cognitive mechanisms.

Over time, we come to associate specific behavioral actions with particular states of mind. These associations eventually become so strong that our mere body movements and positioning can trigger the corresponding cognitive mechanism (Niedenthal et al., 2005). For example, the act of making a fist has become so heavily associated with hostility that men who were subtly influenced to make a fist (under the disguise of a "rock, paper, scissors" type of task) rated themselves as more assertive in a seemingly unrelated questionnaire (Schubert & Koole, 2009).

Now that you have a better "grasp" of embodied cognition, the original three bulleted findings might make more sense:

➤ If a résumé feels heavier—even if it's only due to a heavy clipboard—people falsely associate the heaviness with value. Not only is there a nonsensical belief that more information is packed into the résumé, but there's also the common metaphor that important things tend to "carry more weight."

➤ Why does writing down negative thoughts about yourself lower your self-esteem only when you write them with your dominant hand? When you write down negative thoughts with your nondominant hand, the effect disappears because you're less confident in your writing ability. The lack of confidence that you feel from writing is misattributed to a lack of confidence in the accuracy of those negative thoughts.

➤ When we push our arm upward against a table, that movement resembles bending our arm inward, an action that we perform when we bring something toward us. Because we perform that action when we find something appealing, people who were asked to push their arm upward ate significantly more cookies compared to people who were asked to push their arm downward, an action that we perform when we push something away from us.

As you'll discover in this chapter, embodied cognition is a fascinating phenomenon with tremendous potential.

For those of you who are still biting a pen with your teeth, you can take it out now. Why on earth did I ask you to do that? When you hold a pen in your mouth by biting it with your teeth, this facial positioning causes you to exude the same expressions that you exude when you smile (Strack, Martin, & Stepper, 1988). You're now in a better mood than you were at the beginning of the chapter. The next section will explain why that's the case.

## WHY IS EMBODIED COGNITION SO POWERFUL?

Still skeptical about embodied cognition? There are a few psychological principles that can explain why it occurs.

**Facial Feedback Hypothesis.** Remember how I asked you to read the opening description while biting a pen with your teeth? A group of researchers asked people to view a series of cartoons while holding a pen in their mouth. They asked some people to bite the pen with their teeth, and they asked other people to simply hold the pen with their lips. The researchers found that people who were biting the pen with their teeth (a position that caused them to smile) found the cartoons more amusing compared to people who were holding the pen with their lips (a position that didn't cause them to smile) (Strack, Martin, & Stepper, 1988).

To explain that phenomenon—which has become known as the *facial feedback hypothesis*—Robert Zajonc proposed a *vascular theory of emotion*, a theory suggesting that our body language can trigger biological mechanisms that, in turn, influence our emotional state and interpretation of information. When he and his colleagues (1989) asked German students to repeat certain vowel sounds (*i, e, o, a, u, ah, ü*), they found that students exhibited lower forehead temperature when they repeated *e* and *ah* vowel sounds (sounds that caused them to exude smiling expressions). Those smiling expressions cooled the students' arterial blood, which produced a more pleasant mood by lowering their brain temperature. Conversely, repeating *u* and *ü* sounds forced students to frown, which decreased blood flow and heightened brain temperature, thereby dampening their mood. The mere act of smiling can spark biological mechanisms, which can then trigger attitudes and emotions that we associate with smiling.

Even if particular body language doesn't directly trigger biological responses that alter our mood (e.g., smiling lowers brain temperature, which enhances our mood), our body language can still influence cognitive mechanisms because of self-perception theory.

**Self-Perception Theory.** *Self-perception theory* proposes that we sometimes infer our attitudes by examining our behavior (Bem, 1972). If we hold an ambiguous attitude toward something, we try to make sense of that attitude by examining our actions and body language. For example, when people viewed photographs of celebrities, they perceived them to be less famous when they were asked to view the pictures while furrowing their eyebrows, a facial expression associated with exerting mental effort (Strack & Neumann, 2000). When people furrowed their eyebrows, they inferred from their facial expression that they were exerting mental effort to think of that celebrity, an inference that led them to perceive the celebrities to be less famous.

If there's ever inconsistency between our attitudes and body language, we tend to trust the latter. Consider a clever experiment from the 1960s (Valins, 1967). A researcher told a group of males that he would be measuring their heartbeats in response toward sexual images and that they would be hearing their heartbeat while viewing the photos. However, the men were told that this audio was merely due to poor equipment and that they should ignore the sound of their heartbeat (you should keep in mind that this study was conducted in 1967, when technology was just *slightly* less developed . . .).

During the experiment, the men were shown 10 pictures of females from *Playboy*, and they heard their "heartbeat" increase on 5 of those 10 pictures (when in actuality, the sound was fake and controlled by the researcher). The results were quite surprising: the men found the females more attractive when their heart rate had supposedly increased. This influence was so strong that the males *still* chose those same photographs when they were asked again 2 months later. Thus, even when biological responses are inaccurate (or even fake), we still tend to trust that feedback by developing attitudes that are congruent with those responses. As you'll learn in the next chapter, self-perception theory plays an even more powerful role when it comes to behavior (i.e., not just body language).

## PERSUASION STRATEGY: CONTROL BODY LANGUAGE

Due to our tendency to associate certain body language with certain attitudes (e.g., we associate head nodding with open-mindedness), this section proposes that getting your target to exude certain body language can cause your target to develop certain attitudes that would be favorable for your persuasion. In the following sections, you'll learn some specific types of body language that would be favorable for you to extract, and you'll learn some clever techniques to subtly extract that body language from your target.

**Head Nodding.** With a few rare exceptions (e.g., some parts of India and Africa), head nodding is a widespread symbol for agreement. When people are engaged in a conversation, they'll occasionally nod their head to show that they're interested in what the other person is saying, and it serves as a nonverbal cue for the speaker to continue talking. Due to this heavy association with agreement, getting your target to nod his head before you make your request can trigger a more agreeable and open-minded attitude.

Supporting that claim, Wells and Petty (1980) gave students a pair of headphones and asked them to listen to a radio broadcast. They asked the students to test the quality of the headphones by either nodding their head up and down or by shaking their head from side to side while listening to the broadcast. The researchers found that, compared to students who shook their head from side to side, students who tested the sound quality by nodding their head developed a greater positive attitude toward the message in the broadcast. Due to the strong association between head nodding and agreement, getting people to nod their head before you make your request can trigger a more agreeable state of mind.

How can you get your target to nod her head? Luckily, head nodding is a type of gesture that's fairly easy to nonverbally extract. Whenever you're speaking to someone, you can usually pause or raise your eyebrows to nonverbally communicate when you want that person to acknowledge one of your points, which can then trigger a head nod.

During the moments leading up to your actual request, you should make several of those nonverbal cues for acknowledgement so that you can condition your target to nod her head. Not only would her attitude become more open-minded because of embodied cognition, but those frequent head nods will also trigger a form of inertia. If you condition your target to nod her head multiple times before you make your request, she'll feel motivated to remain consistent with those responses by making an affirmative response to your request (the psychology behind that concept is explained in the next chapter).

**Exposed Chest.** Uh-oh. You're a store clerk, and a robber just busted through your door and pointed a gun at you. What would be your initial reaction? Most people in this situation would immediately react by throwing their arms into the air with their palms pointed outward. When people want to communicate that they're open and they have nothing to hide, they often hold their palms outward with their arms spread to reveal their chest.

Likewise, when people feel closed-minded, they often cross their arms or hold an object in front of them to block their chest. People often block their chest when they're feeling defensive or closed-minded because it serves as a symbolic defense to prevent new information from penetrating their thoughts and attitudes.

If you watch a video of Nixon's speech when he defends himself against the Watergate scandal, after he says, "I'm not a crook. I've earned everything I've got," he immediately steps back from the podium and crosses his arms in front of his chest, as if he wanted to make that statement and retreat without any further questions or inquiries. It reminds me of a child who insults one of his peers and then immediately plugs his ears to prevent his friend from making a "comeback."

Because we associate crossing our arms with greater defensiveness, this position can trigger an unyielding attitude (Bull, 1987). In fact, people in one study were able to solve significantly more anagrams when they were induced to cross their arms because that body language triggered a more persistent attitude (Friedman & Elliot, 2008). Although persistency is typically considered a positive trait, a persistent attitude will dramatically reduce your chances of gaining compliance because you'll be less likely to change someone's attitude.

Instead of combating that persistency, it would be much more favorable for you to wait until your target's body language is more conducive for persuasion. Because an exposed chest (e.g., no crossed arms, no objects being held) triggers a more agreeable attitude, that type of body language *can* enhance your persuasion. Rather than make your request while your target is holding an object (e.g., texting on her phone), you should wait until her hands are empty and her chest is exposed (e.g., her arms aren't crossed).

**Posture.** Finally, your target's posture is another form of body language that can trigger a more favorable attitude. Although not necessarily connected to open-mindedness, there are a few types of attitudes associated with posture that can help enhance your persuasion.

Perhaps the strongest attitude associated with posture is pride. Whenever we feel accomplished or proud, we tend to exude an upright posture, but whenever we feel nervous or insecure, we tend to exude a slumped posture. Research shows that extracting these positions can, in fact, trigger those corresponding attitudes. In one study, Stepper and Strack (1993) measured people's level of satisfaction with their performance on an achievement test, but due to the seating arrangements, people were seated in either an upright or slumped position. The researchers found that, upon discovering their scores, people who were seated upright were significantly more satisfied with their score compared to people who were seated in a slumped position.

In addition to being associated with pride, however, posture is also closely associated with power. If you're familiar with the card game blackjack, then you probably know that people who have 16 are usually unsure if they should play it safe by staying at 16 or by taking a risk and asking for another card in hopes that the new card doesn't put them over 21. The strong association between posture and power can explain why people who are induced to display an expansive body posture are significantly more likely to take another card in that situation (Huang et al., 2011). The expansive posture triggers a congruent attitude associated with power, which nonconsciously influences people to take that risk.

If you're ever feeling nervous or insecure in a particular situation, you can help alleviate those feelings by changing your posture. If you sit upright and exude an expansive posture, you can trigger a congruent attitude of confidence and overcome your nervousness.

To summarize the chapter, we often infer our attitudes from our body language. If you want to instill a certain attitude in your target, you simply need to get your target to exude body language associated with the attitude that you're trying to instill. By getting your target to display that body language, you can trigger an attitude that's "congruent" with that body language.

Although the information in this chapter is powerful, let's be honest, it's not *that* practical. But I still wanted to include this chapter so that you had a good grasp of self-perception theory because the next chapter will explain the more powerful and practical applications of that concept. Specifically, it'll explain why behavior—not just body language—can trigger congruent attitudes. You'll also learn why we feel tremendous pressure to maintain attitudes that are consistent with our behavior and how you can take advantage of that innate desire for consistency.

# CHAPTER 5

# Create Behavioral Consistency

"I don't sing because I'm happy. I'm happy because I sing."
—William James, renowned psychologist

Congratulations! You've just been recruited to participate in an exciting research study.

What are your tasks? First, you'll be given a half hour to place 12 little wooden cylinders onto a tray. You'll probably finish that within a few seconds, but don't worry. Once you finish, you should empty the tray and keep repeating that same process for 30 minutes.

But if that task isn't exciting enough, your second task is even better! After you fill, empty, and refill that tray for a half hour, you'll then be given a board with 48 square pegs. What's your task this time? You need to turn those square pegs a quarter turn each, one at a time, and you should keep repeating that process for another half hour. Aren't you thrilled to be participating in such an exhilarating experiment?

Although a few people might find those tasks enjoyable, it's safe to assume that 99.99 percent of people would find those tasks painfully dull. But here's a question. What if the researchers asked you to convince new participants that the experiment was fun? What if they even paid you for your help? Suppose that you were given either $1 or $20 to convince new participants that the experiment was "fun and exciting." Do you think that your actual attitude toward the experiment would change depending on the reward? If so, in which direction would your attitude change?

In the actual study, people's genuine attitude toward that experiment became significantly more favorable when they were paid $1 (compared to $20) to convince another participant that the experiment was fun (Festinger & Carlsmith, 1959). But how could that be? Common sense suggests that a larger reward should produce a larger attitude change. Why did $1 produce a more favorable attitude toward the experiment compared to $20? This chapter will explain the interesting principle behind that surprising result and how you can use it to persuade other people.

## THE POWER OF (IN)CONSISTENCY

Let's take a moment to travel back in time. In 1954, a rising cult group predicted that a massive flood would occur on December 21 and that it would destroy the entire planet. Fortunately, the leader of the cult claimed that a being from the planet Clarion informed her that a flying saucer would rescue members of her cult on the night before the flood. Phew.

When December 21 came and went without any flood, what do you think happened to members of that cult? Most people today would assume that, once cult members realized that their prediction was wrong, they would probably admit that their belief about the end of the world was also wrong. But is that what they did? Nope. In fact, they did the opposite. When faced with the earth-shattering reality that the flood didn't occur as predicted, the leader of the cult merely changed the date of the flood's arrival, and members actually became *more* committed to the cult. Astonishingly, their beliefs about the flood became even *stronger.*

Unbeknownst to members of the cult who were waiting for the flying saucer to arrive, Leon Festinger, a prominent researcher in social psychology, infiltrated the group with his colleagues. They pretended to be followers of the cult so that they could observe their behavior (pretty dedicated researchers, huh?). Upon witnessing cult members develop stronger beliefs about the end of the world after the flood failed to arrive, Festinger developed an important conclusion: people have a powerful psychological need to maintain consistent attitudes and behavior.

That conclusion can help explain why body language can trigger congruent attitudes. If we display certain body language (e.g., head nodding), and if that body language is inconsistent with our inner attitude (e.g., we're in disagreement), we feel a state of discomfort known as *cognitive dissonance*, and we become motivated to resolve that discomfort. How do we resolve it? We often resolve that dissonance by changing our attitude so that it matches our behavior (e.g., we change our attitude from disagreement to agreement to match our body language of nodding our head).

This chapter expands that knowledge by explaining how that principle occurs not just with body language, but also with behavior. If you start to observe your own daily actions, you'll soon notice that we're influenced by cognitive dissonance nearly every day. Whenever we perform an action that's inconsistent with one of our attitudes, we feel discomfort and we become motivated to resolve that discomfort in some way:

➢ You just started a new diet, yet you're eating a piece of cake. You might justify your inconsistent behavior by reminding yourself that it's your friend's birthday and that it would be "rude" if you didn't eat the cake.

➢ You believe that people shouldn't steal, yet you illegally download music. You might justify your inconsistent behavior by claiming that "everyone else is doing it."

➢ You consider yourself a studious college student, yet you're choosing to hang out with friends rather than study for an exam. You might justify your inconsistent behavior by reassuring yourself that it's your senior year so you need to enjoy it.

Next time you perform an action that's inconsistent with one of your attitudes, pay attention to the little voice inside your head that tries to justify your behavior. That little voice is your attempt to resolve cognitive dissonance.

## WHY IS (IN)CONSISTENCY SO POWERFUL?

The important takeaway from the previous section is that whenever our attitudes and behavior are inconsistent, we become motivated to resolve that inconsistency. This section will explain why that occurs and why behavior, in addition to body language, can trigger congruent attitudes to resolve that inconsistency.

Now, why on earth did those cult members experience such tremendous pressure to maintain their belief about the end of the world? You can start to see the underlying reason when you look at how they acted before the flying saucer failed to arrive. Upon their initial discovery that the world would supposedly end, many cult member displayed behavior consistent with a belief in the end of the world (e.g., many had quit their jobs, sold their possessions, etc.).

On December 21, when cult members realized that the flying saucer didn't arrive as predicted, their belief was challenged. However, to accept the idea that the world wasn't ending would be profoundly inconsistent with their original behavior. In order to overcome that dissonance and discomfort, they needed to do something. And because they couldn't alter their past behavior, they changed the one thing that they *could* change: their attitude. Upon discovering that the flying saucer didn't arrive, most cult members developed stronger beliefs in the end of the world so that they could justify their original behavior.

When the undercover researchers witnessed that surprising outcome, they tested that principle by conducting the experiment described in the beginning of the chapter (Festinger & Carlsmith, 1959). In their experiment, they paid people who just completed a boring experiment either $1 or $20 to lie to new participants and claim that it was fun. Thus, people were asked to perform a behavior that was inconsistent with their inner attitude.

The researchers wanted to examine how that inconsistency would influence their actual attitude toward the experiment, and the results revolutionized beliefs about human behavior. During that era, psychologists believed that greater rewards always led to greater attitude changes, but Festinger and Carlsmith's study disputed that claim by demonstrating how a smaller reward can sometimes lead to a greater attitude change.

Now that you're more aware about cognitive dissonance, you can probably start to guess why people developed a more positive attitude toward the experiment when they were paid $1 to lie to the new participants. When people were asked to lie by claiming that the experiment was fun, they performed a behavior that was inconsistent with their attitude, and thus they experienced dissonance and became motivated to resolve that discomfort. How did they resolve it? Much like the cult members, people in the experiment couldn't change their behavior (i.e., their participation in the experiment), so they changed the only thing that they could change: their attitude toward the experiment.

People who were paid $1 regained consistency and resolved their dissonance by genuinely developing a more positive attitude toward the experiment. If they held a positive attitude toward it, then their behavior of telling the new participant that the experiment was "fun" would be consistent with that attitude.

But wait! What about the $20 group? In that study, people who were paid $20 to lie to new participants didn't develop *any* positive attitudes toward the experiment. What gives! Why did the $1 group find the experiment enjoyable, while the $20 group still thought the experiment was painfully boring?

That difference occurred because people who were paid $20 could more easily justify why their behavior was inconsistent. When people were paid $20, there was a specific reason for their inconsistency (i.e., a large reward), and so they didn't experience as much discomfort because they could easily attribute their inconsistent behavior to the large compensation. However, when people were only paid $1 to lie to the new participant, this small compensation wasn't substantial enough to justify their inconsistent behavior, and so they experienced stronger discomfort and a stronger need to resolve that discomfort.

Here's the main takeaway. Whenever an attitude is inconsistent with our behavior, we feel a state of discomfort known as cognitive dissonance, and we become motivated to resolve it. Further, our motivation to resolve that discomfort becomes stronger when the reason for our inconsistency is weak (e.g., a small reward). If we have a valid reason for holding an inconsistent attitude (e.g., a large reward), we won't feel as much pressure to change our attitude to match our behavior because we can easily justify our inconsistency.

This concept stems beyond just rewards; punishments and threats to display certain behavior also won't influence people to develop a congruent attitude. In another classic experiment, Aronson and Carlsmith (1963) told children that they couldn't play with a desirable toy. The researchers told some children that there would be a severe punishment if they played with the toy (e.g., "I will be very angry, and I will have to pack my toys and go home"), but other children were told that there would only be a mild punishment (e.g., "I will be annoyed"). Although the children in each condition followed the researcher's request by not playing with the toy, what do you think happened when those children encountered that same toy at a later occasion when there was no punishment for playing with it?

You guessed it. Children who received only a mild threat continued to refrain from playing with the toy. Why? The original mild threat was too weak to justify their inconsistent attitude and behavior (i.e., there was a desirable toy in front of them, but they weren't playing with it). Instead, the children resolved their inconsistent behavior by developing a congruent attitude that they simply didn't like the toy. Therefore, when presented with that same toy again, they didn't want to play with it because they genuinely believed that they disliked it. On the other hand, children who received the severe threat could easily attribute their inconsistent behavior (i.e., not playing with the toy) to that large threat. From their perspective, they weren't playing with the toy because of the severe threat, not because they disliked the toy.

Therefore, when those children encountered that same toy again, they were more likely to play with it because they never developed a congruent attitude of disliking the toy.

Researchers often refer to that phenomenon as "insufficient justification" (Shultz & Lepper, 1996). In order for people to develop a congruent attitude—whether it's from their body language or behavior—they must believe that they are freely choosing their behavior, rather than being guided by some large external reward or threat. Too much justification won't lead to cognitive dissonance because people could easily attribute their inconsistent attitude and behavior to that justification. Remember this concept because it'll come back into play when we discuss incentives in Chapter 12.

## PERSUASION STRATEGY: CREATE BEHAVIORAL CONSISTENCY

The main persuasion strategy is very simple (yet extremely powerful). If you want to persuade people to develop a certain attitude, you should get them to display behavior that's consistent with the attitude that you're trying to elicit. When they display that particular behavior, they're more likely to develop an attitude that's congruent with their behavior. This section will explain a few strategies that apply that concept.

**Foot-in-the-Door Technique.** Popularized by Robert Cialdini (2001), the *foot-in-the-door technique* can be a powerful persuasion tactic. When you need to persuade people to comply with a somewhat large request, you can put the odds in your favor by first asking them to comply with a smaller request.

Because you're more likely to gain their compliance with a smaller request, that initial compliance will cause them to develop a congruent attitude that suggests they are the type of person who would help you. When you later ask them to perform the larger request, they'll be more likely to comply with it because they'll feel pressure to remain consistent with their congruent attitude. Not complying with the larger request would be inconsistent with their new attitude, and so many people avoid that discomfort by maintaining consistency and complying with the larger request.

The classic study that initially examined this principle can shed some more light (Freedman & Fraser, 1966). Under the guise of volunteer workers, two researchers tried to influence households to comply with a fairly large request: to install a large and ugly sign declaring "Drive Carefully" in their front yard. When they presented the request alone, the researchers were only able to influence 17 percent of people to comply. Since most people immediately rejected that type of odd and inconvenient request, how did the researchers manage to influence 76 percent of people in another group to comply?

A few weeks before asking those people to install the large sign, the researchers asked them to instead comply with a smaller request: to install a small 3-inch sign that declared "Be a safe driver." Nearly everyone who was asked to install that small sign complied because it was such a minor request. But despite that seemingly insignificant favor, households that complied with this small request became much more likely to install the larger sign when the researchers presented that request a few weeks later. Complying with the small request caused those people to develop a congruent attitude that reflected a person who cares about safe driving. Therefore, when presented with the request to install the large sign a few weeks later, those people felt pressure to install the large sign to maintain consistency.

Was "caring about safe driving" the only attitude that people developed by complying with the smaller request? What if the researchers had presented an initial small request that was unrelated to safe driving? It turns out that small requests, even if they're unrelated, can still lead to future compliance. For some households in the previous study, the researchers asked them to either sign a petition about the environment or to install a small sign that declared "Keep California Beautiful." Although the researchers gained the highest degree of compliance (76 percent) when they presented a similar request and topic (i.e., a small sign about safe driving and then a larger sign about safe driving), they still managed to garner roughly 50 percent compliance when the topic was completely different (i.e., a petition or small sign about keeping California beautiful and then a large sign about safe driving). The topic about keeping California beautiful may not have elicited an attitude about safe driving, but it succeeded in eliciting congruent attitudes that reflected a person who takes pride in her community or who simply does kind favors for strangers.

**Lowball Procedure.** In addition to using a small request to secure compliance with a separate larger request, you could also start with a small request, and once you gain the initial compliance, you can increase the size of that same request.

This *lowball procedure* is a frequent tactic used by salespeople to influence their customers (Cialdini, 2001). In fact, you may have fallen prey to this tactic by a salesperson at a car dealership where this tactic is often used. You just negotiated a great deal with a car salesperson, and as he goes into the back office to write up the paperwork, you rejoice at having secured a fantastic bargain for your new car. In reality, however, the salesperson is probably twiddling his thumbs in the back room, waiting for time to pass so that you have a few moments to fantasize about your new car.

After a few minutes pass, the salesperson returns with some unfortunate news: the manager didn't approve the sale, and the fantastic "bargain" just increased by $500. However, by that point, the salesperson already sparked your momentum by gaining your initial compliance, and as a result, you will feel inertia pushing you toward continued compliance with that enlarged request. You've already fantasized about your new car, and you've already engaged in behavior that suggested you want that car. Much like a puppeteer pulling the string of a marionette, that salesman just pulled the string of cognitive dissonance to pull you toward accepting that enlarged request.

**Suggest an Attitude.** Rather than try to get your target to display certain behavior in order to trigger a congruent attitude, you can accomplish the same goal by subtly influencing your target to commit to holding a particular attitude. Getting him to outwardly claim that he's in a pleasant mood, for example, can elicit behavior that's consistent with a pleasant mood.

How can you elicit that type of claim? It's easier than you might think. Whenever we run into somebody, the first thing that we usually say is "How are you?", and 99 times out of 100, this standard question is usually met with a "good" or "fine." That's just the social norm to which we've become accustomed. Someone could literally be having the worst day of his life, yet he would still probably make one of those standard responses.

Despite that seemingly innocent and automatic response, outwardly committing to holding a "good" attitude can make someone more likely to comply with a request. Once that "good" attitude is publicly known, that person will feel pressure to act in ways that are consistent with a positive attitude, such as complying with a request.

I know what many of you are thinking right now (I'm a mind reader, remember?). You're thinking that we're so accustomed to responding with a "good" or "fine" that those statements have lost their actual meaning; they're so automatic that they aren't strong enough to actually change our attitude, let alone change our behavior and likelihood of complying with a request. You'd think so, but research tells us otherwise. In a study examining that particular strategy, Daniel Howard (1990) phoned residents of Texas and asked them if a representative from the Hunger Relief Committee could visit them to sell cookies. Among residents who were asked only that request, 18 percent agreed. However, among residents who were first asked "How are you feeling this evening?" and who answered with an affirmative response (e.g., "good" or "fine"), the percentage of people who complied nearly doubled to 32 percent. Residents were more likely to comply because they felt pressure to remain consistent with the positive attitude that they claimed to possess. The takeaway: next time that a police officer pulls you over, make sure to ask him how he's doing that day.

# REAL WORLD APPLICATION: HOW TO DRIVE TRAFFIC FROM YOUTUBE VIDEO DESCRIPTIONS

To see how you could begin applying self-perception theory, cognitive dissonance, and congruent attitudes, consider the description that I use for my YouTube videos about mind reading. The descriptions that I currently use (as of September 2013) resemble the following:

———————————— [video above] ————————————

Want to learn the secret . . .

I developed a way to subconsciously influence people's thoughts. Want to learn how? I explain the fascinating method in the first chapter of my book, Methods of Persuasion.
Amazon: [link to my book]
(the eBook is only $4.99)


\*\*\*\*\*\*\*\*\*\*\*\*\*\*\*\*\*\*\*\*\*\*\*\*\*\*\*\*\*\*\*\*\*\*\*\*\*\*\*\*\*\*\*\*\*\*\*\*\*\*\*\*\*\*

My name is Nick Kolenda, and I'm a professional mind reader and psychology researcher. Want to learn more . . .

Blog: www.NickKolenda.com
Facebook: www.facebook.com/mentalismshow
Twitter (new): www.twitter.com/nickkolenda

———————————— [description ends] ————————————

It might seem like an innocent description, but it contains several psychological principles that add more pressure for viewers to purchase my book.

Did you notice how the first rhetorical question ("Want to learn the secret . . .") is spaced apart from the rest of the description? When people watch the YouTube video, that sentence is the only thing that's visible to them in the description. In order to view the rest of the description, people need to physically click on the button that says, "Show More."

Why is that important? When people mentally answer that first rhetorical question with a "yes," they start developing a congruent attitude that reflects someone who wants to learn the secret, and they start to feel pressure to act in a manner consistent with that attitude. Once they click "Show More" to see the rest of the description, that action is a behavioral response that reinforces their attitude, and so their desire to learn the secret becomes even stronger. When they reach the next rhetorical question ("Want to learn how?"), most people would mentally answer that question with another affirmative response, which *further* reinforces their congruent attitude.

At this point, they just experienced three instances that instilled an attitude of someone who wants to learn the secret. When they continue reading the description and see the link to purchase my book, they'll feel pressure to at least click on the link to maintain consistency with their attitude (and clicking that link serves as a fourth instance that reinforces their new attitude). With all of this momentum, people will feel more pressure to maintain that attitude by actually purchasing the book.

# STEP 3

# Trigger Social Pressure

| Before the Request | Step 1: | M | Mold Their Perception |
| | Step 2: | E | Elicit Congruent Attitudes |
| | **Step 3:** | **T** | **Trigger Social Pressure** |
| | Step 4: | H | Habituate Your Message |
| During the Request | Step 5: | O | Optimize Your Message |
| | Step 6: | D | Drive Their Momentum |
| After the Request | Step 7: | S | Sustain Their Compliance |

## OVERVIEW:
## TRIGGER SOCIAL PRESSURE

Now that you've molded your target's perception and elicited a relevant congruent attitude, there's another step to implement before presenting your actual request.

To maximize the amount of pressure that you place on your target, you should trigger some type of social pressure. Nearly every book about influence and persuasion explains the importance of social pressure. Why? Because it's incredibly effective at changing behavior.

Whether we realize it or not, we frequently (as in, every day) decide our own behavior by looking to other people. If everyone is displaying a certain type of behavior, we feel a natural urge to engage in that same behavior. This third step in METHODS will teach you how to leverage that innate tendency so that you can exert more pressure on your target. The first chapter within this step teaches you how to use the power of social norms and group behavior, and the second chapter narrows that focus by explaining how you can harness the power of interpersonal pressure and build greater individual rapport.

# CHAPTER 6

# Emphasize Social Norms

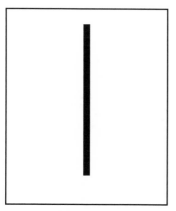

**Standard Line**

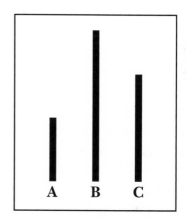

**Comparison Lines**

Look at those lines. If you had to guess, which line among the Comparison Lines is equal to the Standard Line? Is it A, B, or C?

It's B, right? Why would I even bother asking such an obvious question? If the answer is so obvious, then why did 76 percent of people in a research study get that question wrong? Did the researchers receive an unlucky sample of blind people, or were those answers influenced by some psychological force? Since you're reading this book, you can probably guess that it's the latter. This chapter will explain that psychological force, why it's so powerful, and how you can use it to enhance your persuasion.

## THE POWER OF SOCIAL PRESSURE

Now, why did so many people get that question wrong? Solomon Asch, a prominent researcher in social psychology, conducted this ground-breaking study in the 1950s. Asch (1951) wanted to examine the extent to which people conform, and what he found sparked a new a sensation in psychology.

In the experiment, seven people were seated in a row, and they were shown the same lines that you were shown at the beginning of the chapter. The setup and seating arrangement resembled the following:

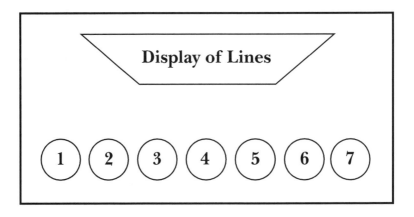

Imagine that you were the person seated in the 6th position. Starting with the person seated in the 1st position, the experimenter asked each of you to verbally answer the "simple" question (i.e., which line among the Comparison Lines is equal to the Standard Line),

Before the person in the 1st position answers, you immediately recognize that B is the correct answer. You might even think that the researcher is crazy for asking such a simple question. That's why when the 1st person answers "C", you're caught off guard. Oh well. You're not too worried because you're confident that the person in the 2nd position will recognize that B is the correct answer.

Unfortunately, that's not what happens. When the 2nd person confirms "C", your small worry quickly turns to panic. What do you do now? Did you miss something? You scrutinize the lines again trying to spot something that you might have missed, but time is running out. Before you have time to rethink your answer, people seated in the 3rd, 4th, and 5th position all answer with a resounding "C." Uh-oh. It's now your turn. What would you do in this situation? Would you stick with your original answer, B? According to the results of the experiment, you probably wouldn't.

In the actual study, the person seated in the 6th position was the only true participant in the study; everyone else was a confederate hired by Asch. The confederates were instructed to give incorrect answers to put social pressure on the person seated in the 6th position, and that social pressure was more powerful than many researchers had estimated. Despite a painfully obvious answer, an astonishing 76 percent of people conformed and gave the same incorrect answer to the question. The next section will expand on this psychological force and explain two reasons why it's so powerful.

## WHY IS SOCIAL PRESSURE SO POWERFUL?

This section will describe the two main reasons why we succumb to social pressure: informational influence and normative influence.

**Informational Influence.** First, we sometimes conform to the beliefs and behavior of others because we come to believe that our own beliefs are incorrect. If the crowd's opinion contradicts our own opinion, then we start to question the accuracy of our own belief, a tendency that becomes even stronger when the correct answer is ambiguous.

Unlike Asch's experiment where the answer was obvious (which triggered normative influence, to be explained next), situations that don't offer a clear and definitive answer will trigger informational influence because we come to distrust our own belief.

Consider another classic experiment on conformity where the answer was more ambiguous. In the 1930s, Muzafer Sherif (1936) examined the influence of social pressure on people's perception of the autokinetic effect, an optical illusion where a small light *seems* to move if the surrounding environment is completely dark (a stationary light in darkness will seem to move because there's no reference point that people can use to keep track of it).

In the experiment, people were placed alone in a dark room, where a small light was presented 15 feet in front of them. The light flashed for two seconds, and people were asked to estimate how far it moved (even though it didn't actually move). The estimates varied widely when people made those estimates alone.

But something interesting happened when people were put in groups of three to make their verbal estimate. When people announced their estimates in groups, the estimates gradually converged over trials. For example, the estimate of the first flash may have elicited answers of 1 inch, 3 inches, and 8 inches from the three people. The estimates of the second flash, however, would have elicited estimates of 2 inches, 3 inches, and 5 inches. Likewise, the estimate of the third flash would show an even greater convergence of perhaps 3 inches, 3 inches, and 4 inches. With each new trial, the estimates from the three people always converged toward an average estimate.

When the answer to a question is unclear or ambiguous, people conform because they're unsure of the correct answer. Upon hearing other people's estimates of the movement of light, people started to question the accuracy of their own estimate, and so they gradually adjusted their estimates to more closely match the estimates from the other people.

How can we be sure that people changed their internal belief about the light movement and that they didn't just give a new estimate to avoid appearing deviant? People were retested alone after the group trials, and their estimates remained near the same converged level that was produced in the group trial (Sherif, 1936). Although informational influence occurs when an answer is unclear or ambiguous, it's replaced by normative influence when the answer is more obvious.

**Normative Influence.** Perhaps even more powerful than informational influence is normative influence, the pressure to conform to avoid certain social consequences.

Unlike people in Sherif's experiment, people in Asch's experiment with the lines gave an answer that was different from their internal belief not because they distrusted their belief but because they felt pressure to avoid appearing deviant.

In a follow-up experiment, people were told that they arrived late and that they should only write their answer, rather than publicly declare it like the other participants. Despite the exact same conditions, people didn't conform when they were asked to only write their answer because their deviance remained undetected by the others (Asch, 1956). Therefore, not only do we conform to other people due to an internal change in our belief (informational influence), but we can also conform to avoid appearing deviant, which can often lead to social rejection.

Why is social rejection so powerful? From a biological perspective, researchers have recently found that social rejection and physical pain share the same "neural circuitry" (the anterior cingulate cortex) (Eisenberger & Lieberman, 2004). Social rejection is so powerful because it's literally painful.

*Pfft, yeah right,* you may be thinking. *If social rejection was physically painful, then I could just pop a Tylenol and feel better.* Well . . . yeah . . . you can. Because social rejection shares the same brain circuitry as physical pain, Tylenol has been found to ease the painful feelings that can result from social rejection (Dewall et al., 2010).

## HOW POWERFUL IS SOCIAL PRESSURE?

Before explaining the specific persuasion strategies, I want to first explain the dangers of determining our behavior based on the behavior of others. Though it doesn't relate directly to persuasion, this section is extremely important. So if you were only half-paying attention . . . *wake up!*

Her name was Kitty Genovese. On March 13, 1964, she was brutally raped and stabbed to death in Queens, New York. What made her death particularly tragic is that it occurred in public. With people nearby. With *many* people nearby. Despite her shrilling cries for help—screams that lasted for 20 minutes—not a single person among the 38 bystanders called the police until 45 minutes later. The police arrived moments after that call, but they were a few minutes too late. Kitty died shortly after they arrived.

How could something so terrible occur in public? Were the bystanders cold and heartless individuals, or was there some psychological force involved? Those questions led a pair of social psychologists, John Darley and Bibb Latané, to explore the latter possibility (Darley & Latané, 1968).

Imagine that you just arrived to participate in a study, and the experimenter explains that you'll be talking to other participants about personal issues via an intercom (because the topics were personal, the intercom would help preserve anonymity). The experimenter even says that he won't be listening over the intercom because he wants to spark genuine conversation, so he mentions that he will only listen to the recording later. But to help keep the conversations organized, only one person will be able to speak into the intercom at a given moment. When someone is done talking, they can then press a button to give another person control of the microphone.

So there you are. You're seated in your own private room, waiting for the other participants to join you over the intercom (for this trial, you're told that you'll only be talking with one other person). Once the other participant joins you, you both start talking about some personal issues. At some point in the discussion, the other person embarrassingly admits that he found it difficult to adjust to college life because he experiences occasional seizures. Albeit interesting and heartfelt, that statement doesn't really faze you until a specific moment later in the discussion.

After the two of you have been talking for a while, the other person is in the middle of talking when he says:

I-er-um-I think I-I need-er-if-if could-er-er-some-
body . . . I-uh-I've got a-a one of the-er-sei er-cr-things
coming on [choking sounds] . . . I'm gonna die-er-er-
I'm . . . gonna die-er-help-er-er-seizure-er-[chokes, then
quiet] (Darley & Latané, 1968, p. 379)

Gulp. Being the only person aware of this potential seizure, what would
you do? Would you go find help? Of course you would. And that's what
happened in the experiment. When people knew that they were the
only person aware of the seizure, nearly everyone immediately left the
room to seek help.

But something dangerously interesting happened when people
believed that more participants were part of the intercom discussion.
In addition to testing 2-person discussions, the researchers sometimes
played recordings of other people over the intercom to make it seem
like other people were participating in the discussion. Some people
were led to believe that they were participating in groups of either 3 or
6 people. What the researchers found shed light on the tragedy with
Kitty Genovese.

When people believed that the discussions included more people,
their likelihood of helping dropped dramatically. When people
believed that they were the only person speaking to the seizure-prone
participant, 85 percent of people left immediately to seek help. However, that percentage dropped to 62 percent in 3-person groups, and
it dropped even further to 31 percent in 6-person groups. With more
people present, the less people felt the need to actively seek help. We
would rather listen to someone having a terrible seizure than to seek
help.

Why are we so heartless? It's not that we're heartless, but rather, it's
because we succumb to two main psychological forces that lower our
tendency to help when there are more people present:

➤ *Diffusion of Responsibility.* In the experiment with the supposed seizure, nearly everyone sprung to action when they believed that they

were the only person aware of the seizure because all responsibility rested on their shoulders. When they believed that more people were part of the discussion, however, responsibility was diffused across those people. With more people present, the less responsibility each individual felt because they assumed that someone else would seek help. With the 38 bystanders near Kitty Genovese's death, they could all hear the rape and murder from inside their apartments, but no one sprung to action and called 911 because they falsely assumed that everyone else had already called.

➤ *Audience Inhibition Effect.* This second explanation stems from a potential embarrassment if we respond to a false "emergency." If someone in the seizure study sought help and the person wasn't actually having a seizure, then that would have felt somewhat embarrassing. People feel inclined not to seek help when a situation is ambiguous so that they can avoid a potential embarrassment. It's truly mind-boggling how a miniscule moment of embarrassment could stand in the way of saving someone's life.

If you remember anything from reading this book, remember this section. The advice in this section could help save your life or the life of someone else. And that's why I wanted to share it before moving on to the other strategies.

Do *not* succumb to social pressure when it comes to helping people. *Always* be an active bystander, even if a situation seems ambiguous. If someone appears to be in trouble, don't diffuse the responsibility to other people. Realize that people are looking to *you* to determine how they should be acting, so if you don't act, other people will be less likely to act. If you see someone lying on the side of a hallway, don't assume that she's sleeping because everyone else keeps walking by. Stop to make sure that she's okay before moving on.

Or if you're ever in trouble yourself, don't make a general plea for help. A general plea will only cause people to diffuse the responsibility. If you're in desperate need of help, you should: (1) directly point to someone so that you destroy her cloud of anonymity within the crowd, and (2) give her a specific and direct request, such as to call 911. This strategy is the proper way to "persuade" someone to help you when the circumstances are dire.

## PERSUASION STRATEGY: EMPHASIZE SOCIAL NORMS

Now that you know the important information surrounding social pressure, how can you use it to persuade other people? This section will describe a few clever techniques to exert that type of social pressure on your target.

**Point Norms in the Desired Direction.** One great benefit about using social norms for persuasion is that a norm can change depending on the situation. If you're in a library where everyone is talking loudly—a behavior that contradicts the typical norm of being quiet—you might assume that the norm in that particular library is more rowdy, and so you would feel less pressure to maintain the norm of talking quietly.

Because social norms aren't set in stone, this flexibility allows you to alter the circumstances to convey a social norm for your particular situation. When researchers examined people's tendency to litter, for example, they found that littering changed in direct proportion with the amount of litter already present. When they increased the pieces of litter on the ground from 1, 2, 4, and 8 pieces, the percentage of people who littered increased from 10 percent, 20 percent, 23 percent, and 41 percent, respectively (Cialdini, Reno, & Kallgren, 1990). With pieces of litter already present, people were more likely to follow the social norm of throwing their trash on the ground, but when fewer pieces of litter were present, people were more likely to follow the social norm of throwing trash into a trash bin.

How can you apply that finding toward persuasion? Let's use tipping and gratuity as an example. If you work in a place where there's a tip jar on the counter, you can exert pressure on your customers to leave larger tips (or *any* tip for that matter) by placing a decent number of dollars in the jar at the beginning of the day. Not only will this money convey a social norm of generous tipping, but the dollars in the jar will also convey that the norm is to tip with dollars, rather than small coins.

If you work in a place where tips are shared among all workers, you can tell everyone how much money you'll be putting in at the beginning of the day and subtract that amount from the total in the tip jar at the end of the day. You'll be surprised how much more money you'll receive from that simple technique.

What if, instead of encouraging behavior, such as generous tipping, you wanted to discourage behavior, such as alcohol use among college students? Emphasizing social norms can help you in those situations as well. Suppose that you were hired by a college committee to post signs discouraging alcohol abuse among students. Between the following two messages, which one do you think would be more effective?

➢ Recent polls suggest that an alarming number of students on this campus abuse alcohol. Please drink safely.
➢ Recent polls suggest that most students on this campus use caution when drinking. Please continue to drink safely.

Extensive research suggests that the second message would be much more effective (Cialdini et al., 2006). The first message has good intentions by trying to emphasize a growing problem, but unfortunately, that type of message can do more harm than good because it points the norm toward the undesired behavior (alcohol abuse).

Whether it's alcohol abuse, suicide, domestic violence, or any other harmful behavior, your attempts to prevent that harmful behavior will be much more effective when you point the norm toward the desired behavior, rather than the harmful behavior. The second statement would be much more effective at reducing alcohol abuse on that campus because it points the norm toward safe drinking, the desired behavior. As Robert Cialdini (2003) describes, "Within the statement

'Many people are doing this *undesirable* thing' lurks the powerful and under-cutting normative message 'Many people *are* doing this.'"

To summarize, when you want to encourage or discourage certain behavior in someone, you should point the norm toward the desired behavior. If you want to increase the size of your tips, demonstrate that most customers tip generously. If you want to discourage alcohol abuse, demonstrate that most students drink safely. Always point the norm in the direction that you want your target to follow.

The next strategy will extend this discussion by explaining one specific and powerful social norm that you can use to add pressure on your target.

**Norm of Reciprocity.** One of the most powerful social norms is reciprocity. There's a reciprocal seesaw connecting us to other people, and it craves balance. When someone does a favor for us, the seesaw gets tilted in our direction, and we feel obligated to do something in return so that the teeter-totter can regain balance. This innate pressure can lead to some very powerful persuasion techniques.

But first, *why* do we feel that pressure? We feel that reciprocal pressure for two reasons. First, by not reciprocating, we're deviating from a social norm, which is an outcome that, as you learned in this chapter, can lead to painful feelings of social rejection. Thus, our reciprocation is our attempt to prevent any painful feelings that may result from the social rejection that occurs from not reciprocating (Cialdini, 2001).

Second, even beyond that superficial motive, we feel an inner sense of obligation. When someone tilts the seesaw in our direction, we feel obliged to return the favor, even if that favor goes unnoticed. Jerry Burger and his colleagues (2009) tested that explanation by creating an experiment that was supposedly testing visual perception, and each trial included two students, unbeknownst to one of them that the other student was a confederate hired by the researchers.

During a designated break, the confederate left and returned with two bottles of water: one for herself, and one for the other student (she explained that the Biology Club was giving them away for free, so she grabbed an extra one). What do you think happened when, at the end of the experiment, the confederate who had given the water bottle asked the participant to fill out a survey for her psychology professor, a favor that was described as completely optional and anonymous (the survey was to be dropped in a box outside the psychology department a few days later, so the confederate would have no idea if the participant actually completed the survey)?

When students were never given a water bottle from the confederate, only 10 percent complied with the request. But when the confederate returned with a water bottle for the participant, the rate of compliance tripled to 30 percent. Even though the confederate would have no idea if the student actually filled out the survey, students who were given a water bottle felt an inner sense of obligation to reciprocate the initial favor. The norm of reciprocity has become so "internalized" that we succumb to its pressure even when we think that no one is looking (Burger et al., 2009).

What are some specific ways to exert that pressure? The following sections will discuss two simple techniques that you can use to tilt the reciprocal seesaw in your target's direction: unsolicited favors and compliments.

*Unsolicited Favors.* Much like the water bottle in the previous experiment, unsolicited favors can trigger a powerful sense of obligation in someone.

Most of us have experienced it. You're sitting in your car, minding your own business, when someone pops out of nowhere and starts washing your window. Pretty annoying, right? Unfortunately, these annoying and unsolicited favors will probably continue for a long time. Why? Because they're incredibly effective at tilting the reciprocal seesaw.

Instead of complaining about those unsolicited favors, why not use them to your advantage? There are endless opportunities to perform small unsolicited favors for people, favors that can trigger a need to reciprocate. The previous strategy explained how leaving dollars in a tip jar can lead to more tips, but what if you only receive direct tips, such as waiters or waitresses? You can increase the size of your direct tips by taking advantage of unsolicited favors. If you perform any type of unsolicited favor for the customers at your table, such as leaving a dinner mint with the check, you put pressure on them to leave a larger tip (Lynn & McCall, 2009).

*Compliments.* Let's face it. People love to be complimented. Granted, you shouldn't recklessly throw compliments at your target for anything and everything. But you also shouldn't hesitate to share genuine respect and praise for a quality that you truly admire about your target.

Compliments not only enhance your likability, but they also tilt the seesaw in your target's direction. When someone compliments you, don't you feel an urge to say or do something nice in return? It's almost an automatic response. If someone compliments your outfit, for example, you'll find yourself scanning that person's clothing, hair, shoes, anything at all that seems appealing so that you can return the favor.

Research even shows that compliments can lead to different forms of reciprocation, not just a reciprocal compliment. For instance, a few research studies have shown that complimenting customers resulted in larger tips, better product evaluations, and higher sales commissions (Seiter & Dutson, 2007; DeBono & Krim, 1997; Dunyon et al., 2010).

If you're a waiter or waitress, a simple compliment toward your customer's food selection (e.g., "I've had that meal before, and it's delicious. Great choice!") can do wonders. There are three reasons, in particular, why that statement is so powerful:

1.  You convey high expectations for the meal. As a result of her heightened expectations, your customer is likely to develop a more favorable perception of the meal (explained in Chapter 3), thereby leading to a more pleasurable overall experience and possibly a larger tip.

2. That simple compliment tilts the reciprocal teeter-totter in your customer's direction, and it will exert greater pressure to give back. What better way to give back than to leave a generous tip?

3. By saying that you also enjoy the meal, you reveal a shared similarity. As you'll learn in the next chapter, revealing this "incidental similarity" can greatly enhance your likability and improve your chances of securing a larger tip.

This chapter explained the power behind social pressure and how you can guide your target's behavior by pointing a social norm in the intended direction (and also by taking advantage of the norm of reciprocity). The next chapter will explain how social pressure can also be applied on an individual level. You'll learn a very powerful principle that can build your rapport and likability to exert even more pressure on your target.

# CHAPTER 7

# Reveal Any Similarities

Among the following letters, pick the letter that you prefer the most:

J    M    L    K

Did you make a choice? I chose the previous letters because they're commonly used as the first letter in people's names (e.g., Joe, Meghan, Lauren, Kevin). If the first letter of your name appears in that list, you were more likely to choose that letter.

This chapter will explain why that occurs and why we nonconsciously gravitate toward things that we perceive to be similar to us. As you'll learn in this chapter, revealing nearly any form of similarity—no matter how small or insignificant it may appear—can tremendously boost your persuasion.

## THE POWER OF SIMILARITIES

If you're reading this book, then you probably find psychology interesting. What a coincidence . . . I love psychology too!

One of the most powerful factors that can influence your chances of gaining compliance is the amount of rapport that exists between you and your target. The more he likes you, the greater your chances of succeeding; the less he likes you, the lower your chances of succeeding. Although the title of this chapter could have been titled, "Build Greater Rapport," the topic of building rapport is extremely broad, so this chapter focuses on explaining the single most effective strategy: emphasizing similarities that you share with your target (for a more comprehensive explanation of rapport-building techniques, refer to Dale Carnegie's classic book, *How to Win Friends and Influence People*).

The old saying, "opposites attract," is almost entirely wrong. Extensive research shows that we're psychologically drawn toward people who resemble ourselves in appearance, interests, and virtually all other aspects. The principle of *incidental similarity* explains how rapport can develop when two people discover a shared similarity, even a small and irrelevant similarity, such as a shared love for psychology (wink wink).

Our psychological compulsion to gravitate toward similarities is so powerful that it can even dictate our lives. How so? In a fascinating study, Pelham, Mirenberg, and Jones (2002) found some peculiar surprises:

➤ People named Dennis are disproportionately more likely to become dentists, and people named George or Geoffrey are disproportionately more likely to work in fields of the geosciences (e.g., geology).

➤ Roofers are 70 percent more likely to have names beginning with the letter *R*, and hardware store owners are 80 percent more likely to have names beginning with the letter *H*.

➤ People named Philip, Jack, Mildred, and Virginia are more likely to reside in Philadelphia, Jacksonville, Milwaukee, and Virginia Beach, respectively.

Needless to say, similarities are another powerful force that nonconsciously guide our behavior.

As you'll learn in the rest of this chapter, this principle extends beyond mere letters. You'll learn why nearly *any* form of similarity that you share with your target can help you build rapport and increase your chances of gaining compliance.

## WHY ARE SIMILARITIES SO POWERFUL?

What make similarities so powerful? This section will describe two explanations that research has offered.

**Evolution.** The first explanation is evolution (Lakin et al., 2003). From an evolutionary perspective, our ancestors were drawn toward others who appeared similar because they seemed less threatening; if someone appeared dissimilar, they needed to exert more caution because they posed a greater threat. People who failed to exert more caution were often killed, and so those types of people were gradually wiped away over time. Because our ancestors were smart enough to realize the importance of similarities, they lived to pass on their adaptive traits, which is why similarities continue to exert tremendous power over us even today.

**Implicit Egotism.** Although evolution is one explanation, the explanation that has garnered the most support is *implicit egotism*, a concept suggesting that we all possess an underlying sense of self-centeredness (Pelham, Carvallo, & Jones, 2005).

Due to our egotistical nature, we possess a hidden psychological urge to gravitate toward things that resemble us in any way. People named Dennis are more likely to become dentists because they developed an affinity toward the letters in their name, and that affinity guided their behavior toward an occupation containing the same letters from their name (Nuttin, 1985).

It might sound ludicrous, but there's ample evidence that shows our profound affinity toward the letters in our name, a concept known as the *name-letter effect*. Research shows that consumers significantly prefer brand names containing the same letters in their name (Brendl, et al., 2005), and this effect is so strong that those brands influence how people consume those products. For example, one study found that people named Jonathan will consume more of a Japanese drink called "Joitoki" (Holland et al., 2009).

Even beyond the name-letter effect, more support for implicit egotism can be found in our failure to recognize our own face. Imagine that someone took a picture of you and manipulated it to make new versions of that picture. Some pictures made you look more attractive, whereas other pictures made you look less attractive. If you were then presented with a line-up of your attractive and unattractive distortions, would you be able to recognize your actual picture? Of course, right? Well, it turns out that it might be harder than you think.

When researchers presented people with a line-up of attractive and unattractive distortions of their face, and when people were asked to choose their own true face, people consistently chose an attractive distortion of their face, rather than their own true face (Epley & Whitchurch, 2008). Our implicit egotism is so strong that we don't even recognize our own face!

## PERSUASION STRATEGY: REVEAL ANY SIMILARITIES

Now that you understand why we gravitate toward similarities, this section will teach you how to use that knowledge to increase your chances of gaining compliance.

**Incidental Similarity.** Because we're psychologically compelled to gravitate toward similar stimuli, you can use this pressure to guide your target toward your intended goal by emphasizing any type of similarity that you share with your target. This *incidental similarity* will help you appeal to his implicit egotism, while building greater rapport and increasing your chances of securing his compliance.

To examine the impact of revealing *any* similarity, Jerry Burger and his colleagues (2004) told people that they were conducting an experiment on astrology. During the astrology-related tasks, participants discovered that they shared the same birthday with a fellow participant (who was actually a confederate working with the researchers). The researchers wanted to see if that incidental similarity would make that person more likely to comply with a request from the confederate.

When people believed that the experiment was finished, they left the room with the confederate and walked down the hall together. While walking, the female confederate asked the participant if he would help her with her English assignment. What was the assignment? She needed to find a student who would review her 8-page essay and write a 1-page critique of her arguments (very far from an enticing request). However, the researchers found that people who discovered that they shared the same birthday with the confederate were significantly more likely to help with that demanding request.

After receiving those startling results, the researchers conducted a follow-up study to understand how the perceived rarity of a similarity fits into the equation. If we discover that we share a similarity with someone, does our propensity to help increase if that similarity is more uncommon?

The researchers examined that question by conducting the same experiment with new participants. This time, however, rather than discovering a shared birthday, participants discovered that they shared a similar fingerprint with the confederate. Some participants were told that the category of that fingerprint was common, whereas other participants were told that the category of the fingerprint was rare.

As expected, the percentage of compliance with the English assignment increased according to the rareness of the fingerprint.

> When people remained unaware that they shared a similar fingerprint, the percentage of compliance was 48 percent.
> When people discovered that they shared a similar yet common fingerprint, the percentage of compliance rose to 55 percent.
> When people discovered that they shared a similar and rare fingerprint, the percentage of compliance rose dramatically to 82 percent.

Although any similarity will make your target more likely to comply with a request, that pressure increases in accordance with the rarity of that similarity. But you should also keep in mind that the similarity doesn't need to be relevant or important, only uncommon (e.g., a rare fingerprint).

How can you apply that principle? If you're meeting your target for the first time, take a moment to learn about her: ask about her life, her interests, and anything else. Not only does this action show interest (another technique to build rapport), but more importantly, it allows you to pinpoint similarities that you might share with your target.

Upon discovering a similarity, don't hesitate to reveal that shared similarity so that you can appeal to her implicit egotism, especially if that similarity is uncommon. Even if the similarities seem irrelevant or unimportant (e.g., a shared first name, mutual friend, similar interest, etc.), those incidental similarities can dramatically boost your persuasion.

You could even use incidental similarity in conjunction with social norms. In one interesting study, Goldstein, Cialdini, and Griskevicius (2008) examined how different messages would encourage hotel guests to reuse their towels. Take a guess which message had the greatest impact:

> ➤ HELP SAVE THE ENVIRONMENT. The environment deserves our respect. You can show your respect for nature and help save the environment by reusing your towels during your stay.
> ➤ JOIN YOUR FELLOW GUESTS IN HELPING TO SAVE THE ENVIRONMENT. In a study conducted in Fall 2003, 75% of the guests participated in our new resource savings program by using their towels more than once.

I'm sure you can guess by now that the second message elicited more compliance because it pointed the norm in the desired direction. And that's exactly what happened. The first message had a compliance rate of 37 percent, whereas the second message had a compliance rate of 44 percent.

But something interesting happened when the researchers tweaked the second message to emphasize a more uncommon similarity:

> ➤ JOIN YOUR FELLOW GUESTS IN HELPING TO SAVE THE ENVIRONMENT. In a study conducted in Fall 2003, 75% of the guests who stayed in this room participated in our new resource savings program by using their towels more than once.

When the researchers described that guests from the same room had reused their towel (a stronger similarity than simply staying at the same hotel), compliance jumped even higher to 49 percent. Why was that small change so profound? The next section will explain why belonging to a perceived "ingroup" can trigger a higher rate of compliance.

**Ingroup Favoritism.** A second application of similarities can be found in *ingroup favoritism*, the tendency for people to prefer groups that share a similar characteristic to themselves. Whether you attend the same school, play on the same sports team, or share the same hotel room, research shows that people generally prefer (and are more persuaded by) members of ingroups. In fact, when we merely view faces of people from an ingroup, there's greater neural activity in our orbitofrontal cortex, the brain region associated with rewards (Van Bavel, Packer, & Cunningham, 2008).

Research shows that we're easily persuaded by members of ingroups and easily dissuaded by members of outgroups. Consider a fascinating experiment. Imagine that you and a stranger are participating in a taste test, and both of you are allowed to take as much food as you want. The stranger takes a certain amount of food and walks away, and you're left standing in front of the food, contemplating how much to take. Researchers found that the amount of food you take would be greatly influenced by the characteristics of the other person and how much food she took (McFerran et al., 2010b).

In that study, the stranger was actually a thin female confederate. In some trials, she was her normal thin self, but in other trials, she wore a professionally-designed prosthesis (a suit that made her look overweight). The researchers wanted to examine how her body type—thin vs. overweight—would influence people's decision about how much food to take, and the results were startling.

The researchers found that people matched the confederate's portion size when she seemed thin, yet they took the opposite portion size when she seemed overweight. When the confederate was thin and took a small portion, people also took a small portion; when she took a large portion, people also took a large portion. But when the confederate appeared overweight, people chose the opposite portion size.

When the confederate seemed overweight and took a large portion, people took a small portion; when she took a small portion, people took a large portion.

What sparked those results? When people appear overweight, they're perceived to be part of a dissociative group, a group from which other people try to "dissociate." People in the previous study took the opposite portion size when they perceived the confederate to be overweight because they felt a nonconscious pressure to distance themselves from her.

But here's a question. What if people in the previous study were on a strict diet? Wouldn't dieters identify with someone overweight because they both share a desire to lose weight? If that were the case, wouldn't the results flip because that similarity would make the confederate part of their ingroup? A second study examined whether that outcome occurs, and, it turns out . . . it does.

In a separate study that used a similar methodology, strict dieters identified with the confederate when she seemed overweight, whereas non-dieters identified more with the confederate when she was thin (McFerran et al., 2010a). In both cases, the dieters and non-dieters showed the greatest amount of persuasion (i.e., chose similar portion sizes) when they could identify with the confederate.

When trying to persuade someone, how can you demonstrate that you belong to the same ingroup? Not only can you use the first technique of revealing any type of similarity, but you could also simply use words like "we" and "us" to reinforce that you belong to the same ingroup. Research shows that these pronouns can trigger a feeling of pleasure because they convey that you belong to the same ingroup (Perdue et al. 1990).

When I was editing this book, I realized that I was explaining many of the psychological principles using 3rd person examples (e.g., "people experience implicit egotism"), and so I went through and changed all of the wording to 1st person examples (e.g., "we experience implicit egotism"). Did it help create rapport between me and you? Who knows. But it definitely didn't hurt.

**Chameleon Effect.** Here's a quick exercise you can try (but you should read this *entire* paragraph first so that you know what to do, and *then* try the exercise). Hold your arms straight out in front of you, parallel to the floor, with your palms facing each other. Put about 3–5 inches of space between your palms, and then close your eyes. Once your eyes are closed, imagine that I placed two powerful magnets on the insides of both your palms, and then imagine that those magnets are pulling your hands together. Use all of your imaginative power to really *feel* those magnets pulling your hands closer toward each other. Do you understand what you're supposed to do? Great. Put the book down and do that exercise for about 30 seconds, and then come back here (by the way, if you skip ahead and read why I'm having you do this exercise, it won't have the same effect if you want to return to try it).

So did you do the exercise? Welcome back. I'm sure that some of you were pretty startled when you felt your hands actually press together. I'm also sure that some of you opened your eyes after a minute with no change in your hand position whatsoever, only a heightened skepticism of this supposed "psychology." And I'm also sure that most of you kept reading without the slightest inclination to try the exercise because you're too resilient to take instructions from a mere book. Well played, my friend.

In any case, whenever I hypnotize someone, I use that exercise to test that person's level of hypnotizability. Though the test is by no means definitive, people who are hypnotizable generally show greater movement in their hands because their imagination causes their hands to move together more easily than people who are not as easily hypnotized.

The underlying principle behind that phenomenon is known as the *ideomotor response,* and it's our tendency to perform behavior upon merely thinking about that behavior. People who are more easily affected by the ideomotor response will exhibit greater movement in their hands when they simply imagine their hands moving closer together. But the ideomotor response also applies to areas beyond mere body movements. For example, thinking about aggression can trigger aggressive behavior (much like priming), which is one of the key reasons why violence in video games and movies can increase aggressive behavior in children (Anderson & Bushman, 2001).

How does this principle relate to similarities? When we speak with people, we examine their nonverbal behavior and experience a hidden psychological urge to mimic that behavior. If someone is speaking with his arms crossed, you may soon find yourself with your own arms crossed. If that person is speaking with an enthusiastic tone, you may find yourself using a similar upbeat tone.

Though it occurs outside of our conscious awareness, this *chameleon effect* is a key element in building rapport (Lakin et al., 2003). Not only do we tend to mimic people that we like, but we also like people more when they mirror our own nonverbal behavior. In fact, researchers found the following outcomes when people imitated nonverbal behavior:

➢ Waitresses gained higher tips (Van Baaren et al., 2003).
➢ Sales clerks achieved higher sales and more positive evaluations (Jacob et al., 2011).
➢ More students agreed to write an essay for another student (Guéguen, Martin, & Meineri, 2011).
➢ Men evaluated women more favorably in speed dating (Guéguen, 2009).

Thus, not only do "incidental similarities" result in a greater likelihood to comply with a request, but so too does similar nonverbal behavior.

In addition to evolution and implicit egotism (the two reasons that were described earlier in the chapter), another reason why similar nonverbal behavior is so powerful can be found in our brain's desire for symmetry. When another person imitates our nonverbal behavior, this symmetry activates the medial orbitofrontal cortex and the ventromedial prefrontal cortex, brain regions that are associated with reward processing (Kühn et al., 2010). Mimicking behavior is so powerful because, in a way, the symmetry is biologically pleasing.

There are two basic strategies you can use to take advantage of this principle. The first should be pretty obvious: to gain compliance, you should build greater rapport by mimicking your target's nonverbal behavior. Commonly used by therapists to convey empathy (Catherall, 2004), this strategy has been implemented in various settings with remarkable success (as you can see in the previous list of experimental outcomes).

Due to the powerful impact of mimicking nonverbal behavior, you should always strive to make your request in person. Although that advice may sound somewhat foreign due to our technology- and e-mail-obsessed society, you're more likely to gain compliance when you make a request in person (Drolet & Morris, 2000). If your situation isn't conducive for an in-person interaction (e.g., far distance), you should use video conferencing or, at the very least, a phone call. The more nonverbal cues that are available, the more easily you can mimic them to build rapport with your target, which will increase your chances of gaining compliance.

To understand the second strategy of mimicry, think back to the concept of congruent attitudes and how we infer our attitudes by observing our body language and behavior. Remarkably, research reveals that we sometimes infer our attitudes by observing the behavior of others who we perceive to be similar to us. Using an EEG (a brain-wave recording device), Noah Goldstein and Robert Cialdini (2007) led people to believe that they shared similar brainwave patterns with a student who appeared in a video interview, an interview that depicted the student's altruistic efforts toward helping the homeless. When the researchers asked participants to complete a questionnaire after watching the interview, people who were informed of the similar EEG patterns not only rated themselves to be more self-sacrificing and sensitive, but they were also significantly more likely to help the researchers in an additional study. People were more likely to assist in the additional study because they observed the altruistic behavior from the supposedly similar student, and they developed a congruent attitude from that student's behavior.

If your target perceives you to be similar, she will develop attitudes that are congruent with *your* behavior. Therefore, if your target perceives you to be similar, you should display behavior that's consistent with the attitude that you're trying to extract from your target. For instance, if one of your close friends is starting to struggle in school, you should make an effort to have occasional study sessions together, even if you're not in the same class. The simple exposure to seeing you study might help your friend develop a genuine interest in studying more, which could help boost her grades. Even if you simply talk about your interest in the material from your class, you could help your friend develop a congruent attitude that she's also interested in the material from her classes.

## A MIND READER'S PERSPECTIVE: HOW TO FREAK PEOPLE OUT USING THE IDEOMOTOR RESPONSE

Want to freak people out? Many psychological principles, such as the ideomotor response, can seem simplistic; but with enough showmanship, you can make these simplistic techniques seem like powerful miracles. This section describes one demonstration that you can use to truly freak people out.

First, find any pendulum type of object (an object attached to the end of a string that will swing back and forth). If you hold the end of the string steady and leave about 8 inches of string for the object to swing freely in the air, you'll find that merely thinking about a direction will cause the object to swing in the direction that you're imagining. If you think about the pendulum swinging left and right, the pendulum will start swinging left and right. If you think about the pendulum swinging forward and back, it'll start swinging forward and back. Because of the ideomotor response, your hand will be making minuscule movements to move the pendulum, but the funny part is that you won't even feel your hand moving at all; it'll seem like you're controlling the pendulum with your mind. It's pretty freaky.

But here's where your showmanship can make this principle seem like a miracle. If you bring a pendulum to your friend, you can describe how that pendulum has certain "powers." To demonstrate, you ask your friend to think of something (let's assume that you ask him to think of a playing card, and let's assume that he thinks of the Jack of Clubs). You instruct him to hold the end of the string so that the attached object hangs freely, and you explain that swinging forward and back means "yes" and that swinging left and right means "no."

After you give these basic instructions, you proceed to ask him yes or no questions about the playing card to narrow down the options, and you tell him to merely think of his answer. When he thinks of his answer, the pendulum will swing in the appropriate direction because of the ideomotor response, but your friend won't realize it. It'll seem like the pendulum is moving on its own.

For example, your first question could be, "Is your card red?" This would cause your friend to think "no" because his card was the Jack of Clubs. If you ask him to concentrate on his answer, the pendulum will start to move a little sporadically, but you'll find that it'll start to move consistently from side to side, indicating a negative answer.

You can then ask additional questions (e.g., is your card a club, is your card a royal card) to narrow down the possibilities. After about five or six "yes" or "no" questions, you can divine the playing card that your friend never even mentioned out loud, and your friend will have no idea that it was the ideomotor response that caused the pendulum to swing in those directions. Though a simple principle, this demonstration can seem like a miraculous phenomenon to people.

# REAL WORLD APPLICATION:
# HOW TO BOOST SALES

In this Real World Application, based on a study by Wansink, Kent, and Hoch (1998), you're a manager at a supermarket, and you decide to use anchoring, limitations (the topic of Chapter 13), and social pressure to boost sales of a particular item.

Near the shelves that display the cans of Campbell's soup, you hang a sign that says, "Limit of 12 per person." Albeit an innocent sign, that statement packs a powerful punch for a few reasons. First, the number 12 sets an anchor that people assimilate toward. Rather than purchase 1 or 2 cans, people are influenced by that anchor to purchase a larger number of cans. Second, as you'll learn in Chapter 13, limiting the ability to purchase those cans will spark "psychological reactance," and it'll spark a greater desire to purchase cans of soup. Third, that sign triggers social pressure by implying that the cans of soup are very popular (why else would the store be limiting the number of cans that people can purchase?).

In the actual study, the researchers included three variations of that sign, and they measured how many cans people purchased with each sign:

- "No limit per person" generated an average of 3.3 cans sold.
- "Limit of 4 per person" generated an average of 3.5 cans sold.
- "Limit of 12 per person" generated an average of 7.0 cans sold.

Remarkably, the original 12-limit sign generated sales that were nearly double those of the other signs.

If you wanted to further enhance the effectiveness of that sign, you could even change the wording to say, "Limit of 12 per customer" or "Limit of 12 per [Supermarket Name] customers." That small wording change takes advantage of ingroup favoritism by emphasizing that people from the same ingroup (i.e., customers) are purchasing those cans of soup. Much like the hotel influenced people to reuse their towels when they emphasized that guests from the same room reused their towels, when you narrow the focus from "person" to "customer" or "[Supermarket Name] customers," you can exert even more pressure on people to purchase those cans of soup (or any other item for that matter).

# Habituate Your Message

| | | | |
|---|---|---|---|
| **Before the Request** | *Step 1:* | **M** | Mold Their Perception |
| | *Step 2:* | **E** | Elicit Congruent Attitudes |
| | *Step 3:* | **T** | Trigger Social Pressure |
| | ***Step 4:*** | **H** | **Habituate Your Message** |
| **During the Request** | *Step 5:* | **O** | Optimize Your Message |
| | *Step 6:* | **D** | Drive Their Momentum |
| **After the Request** | *Step 7:* | **S** | Sustain Their Compliance |

## OVERVIEW:
## HABITUATE YOUR MESSAGE

**ha·bit·u·ate**
To become accustomed or used to something

We're almost there! There's just one final step to implement before you make your actual request. Now that you've molded your target's perception, elicited a congruent attitude, and triggered social pressure, this next step involves habituating your message.

The first chapter in this step will explain why making your target more familiar with your request (via repeated exposures to the general topic) can make that person more likely to comply with your request. The second chapter in this step will explain a clever strategy that uses habituation to desensitize people to any message or request that you know they will find unfavorable. Once you complete this step, the next step will be to present your actual message.

# CHAPTER 8

# Use Repeated Exposures

If you had to guess, which picture of yourself do you think you'd prefer: an actual picture or a picture of your mirrored reflection? I'll give you a few paragraphs to think about it.

When I tried my first beer in college, I thought it tasted disgusting. I hated it. I started arguing with my friends because I thought they were crazy for enjoying the taste. They argued with me by saying that I would eventually learn to like it, but I still thought they were crazy.

It wasn't until my third or fourth beer until I finally realized that my friends were right. Although I initially hated my first few beers, I gradually developed an appreciation for the taste over time, and now I love the taste of beer. How could that be? How could something that I found so disgusting and repulsive become something that I now find very pleasant?

You've probably experienced similar situations in your own life. Have you ever heard a song for the first time that you immediately disliked? Then, after listening to it a few times, you actually begin to enjoy it? How about when you meet someone for the first time? Maybe you dislike him at first, but after meeting him a few times, his personality starts to grow on you? These situations occur frequently, and they can be explained by a psychological principle.

The *mere exposure effect*, also known as the *familiarity principle*, suggests that we develop greater positive feelings toward a stimulus if we're repeatedly exposed to it. The more often you encounter a stimulus (e.g., beer, song, person), the more appealing and likable that stimulus generally becomes. Though it may appear counterintuitive to our current beliefs (such as the popular phrase, "familiarity breeds contempt"), ample evidence has shown that repeated exposures to a stimulus lead to a more favorable perception of that stimulus. This chapter sheds light on why that's the case.

## THE POWER OF REPETITIONS

Now back to my original question: do you think that you would prefer an actual picture of yourself or a picture of your mirrored reflection? Researchers conducted this experiment and found that, if presented with both options, you're more likely to prefer a picture of your mirrored reflection, whereas your friends are more likely to prefer the actual picture of yourself, even when those two images are virtually identical (Mita, Dermer, & Knight, 1977).

If you understand the mere exposure effect, you can understand why those results occurred. Think about it. Each day we wake up, walk into the bathroom, and what do we see? We see our reflection in the mirror. Each day we wake up, walk outside, and what do our friends see? They see us from their own viewing perspective. Therefore, when presented with those two images, people prefer the image that generates the most familiarity. We prefer the picture of our mirrored reflection, and our friends prefer the actual picture because those are the perspectives that generate the most familiarity.

Even if we fail to consciously notice a repeated stimulus, we're still likely to develop positive feelings toward it through nonconscious exposures. In one study, researchers repeatedly flashed geometric shapes to participants, and these shapes were flashed so quickly (4 milliseconds) that participants failed to consciously process them. After those exposures, the researchers presented participants with two shapes: one shape that was previously flashed and one shape that was completely new. The researchers asked them which shape they preferred, and despite absolutely no conscious recognition for the original shape, people consistently chose the shape that the researchers flashed on a nonconscious level (Bornstein, Leone, & Galley, 1987).

In fact, the mere exposure effect is *stronger* when the exposures occur nonconsciously (Zajonc, 2001). How could something that we don't even perceive create a stronger effect? The answer lies in the *affective primacy hypothesis*, a concept suggesting that our emotional responses can be triggered before our cognitive responses. Mere exposure becomes stronger for exposures that occur outside of our conscious awareness because those exposures trigger an emotional response without triggering a cognitive response. They enhance mere exposure because whenever we consciously evaluate something, we attach other meanings and associations to that stimulus, thereby altering (and possibly degrading) our evaluation of it. Nonconscious exposures prevent those potentially harmful associations, and so they often produce more powerful effects than conscious exposures.

Ever since Robert Zajonc proposed the mere exposure effect in the 1960s (Zajonc, 1968), extensive research has investigated this phenomenon, and the results show that this effect applies in many different contexts with many different stimuli. The researchers who conducted the experiment with the geometric shapes conducted a follow-up study and replaced the shapes with pictures of actual people. They found that the results were consistent: participants who were repeatedly exposed to photographs of people on a nonconscious level consistently preferred those photographs over new photographs (Bornstein, Leone, & Galley, 1987). The next section explains why this effect occurs, and the remainder of the chapter will teach you specific techniques to apply that principle toward persuasion.

## WHY ARE REPETITIONS SO POWERFUL?

The previous chapter described how similarities are powerful because of evolution; we're naturally drawn toward people who are similar because they pose less of a threat. The mere exposure effect works in a similar way, no pun intended. Repeated exposures can generate a positive attitude toward a stimulus because they promote a greater sense of familiarity with that stimulus, which makes that stimulus seem less threatening.

Besides evolution, however, there are a few other reasons why the mere exposure effect is so powerful. The two main explanations are classical conditioning and processing fluency (Zajonc, 2001). Because classical conditioning is described in the final chapter, this section will focus on processing fluency, a very interesting principle in psychology.

**Processing Fluency.** It might seem like a strange request, but you'll gain a much better understanding of processing fluency if you take a few minutes to write a list of 12 specific instances in your life where you acted assertively. Go ahead; I'll wait.

Do you have your list? Like most people, you probably thought of a few instances very easily, but with each new example, you probably found it increasingly difficult to think of new instances. Surprisingly, that difficulty in retrieval influenced how you perceived your level of assertiveness. Researchers conducted that same exercise with people, except they asked one group to think of 12 instances, and they asked a different group to think of only 6 instances. What do you think happened when the researchers later asked those people to rate their own assertiveness? Though you might be inclined to think that people who listed 12 instances found themselves to be more assertive, the opposite actually occurred: people who listed only 6 instances viewed themselves to be significantly more assertive than people who listed 12 instances (Schwarz et al., 1991).

The answer to that odd finding can be found in *processing fluency*—the ease and speed with which we process information (Reber, Schwarz, & Winkielman, 2004). If you followed the exercise and listed 12 instances of your assertiveness, you likely experienced difficulty in generating new instances the farther along you went. That perceived difficulty is the answer. The difficulty you experienced in generating new instances became a subtle cue that caused you to develop a congruent attitude that you must not be assertive. You nonconsciously said, "Hmm. If I'm an assertive person, then I should have no problem listing instances. But I *am* having trouble listing instances. Therefore, I must not be assertive." The people who only listed 6 instances, on the other hand, didn't experience as much difficulty generating examples, so their nonconscious developed the opposite attitude: "Hmm. If I'm an assertive person, then I should have no problem listing instances. I'm not having trouble listing instances. Therefore, I must be assertive."

The ease and speed with which we process information largely influences our perception of that information, including how much we like it. Generally, the faster we're able to process information, the more we tend to like that information. Why? When we're able to quickly process information, that ease of processing feels good, and we misattribute the root cause of those positive feelings. When we experience those positive feelings, we mistakenly believe that they are resulting from our fondness for the information, rather than our ease of processing (which is the actual cause).

How does that relate to repetitions? Repetitions are powerful because they increase processing fluency; each time that we view a repeated stimulus, we're able to process that stimulus more quickly the next time we encounter it.

It's like sledding down a snow-covered hill. The first time you try sledding down a hill, you might not slide very fast because the snow won't be compacted. However, each time that you slide down the hill, those repetitions compact the snow and make a smoother pathway down the hill. As the snow becomes more compacted, the smoother your path becomes, and the faster you'll slide down the hill (and the faster you travel, the more you enjoy sledding down the hill).

Think of a time when you might've had the following experience. You start writing an essay and you immediately hate your writing. But after working on it for a few hours, you finally reach a point where you're pleased with it, and so you take a break for the rest of the day. When you return to it the next day, however, you find that you hate it again. Why is that?

The answer lies in processing fluency. You disliked the writing initially because your processing fluency was low; it was still foreign to you. But the more you worked on it, the more familiar it became, and the easier it became to process. You then misattributed the ease with which you processed it with your fondness for the writing. When you took a break from it, your processing fluency decreased, and because it wasn't as familiar to you when you returned to it, you weren't able to process it as easily. You then misattributed that difficulty in processing to a poor essay.

Now that you understand processing fluency and why repetitions are so powerful, the next section explains how you can use that concept to enhance your persuasion.

## PERSUASION STRATEGY: USE REPEATED EXPOSURES

How can you take advantage of repetitions? This section offers a few suggestions.

**Prime the Context.** How pleasant do you find the word "boat"? It may seem like a weird question, but when researchers in one study asked people that same question, they found some interesting results. Compare the following two sentences that the researchers presented to two groups of people:

➢ He saved up his money and bought a boat.
➢ The stormy seas tossed the boat.

The researchers presented those two sentences to people and asked them to focus solely on the last word (i.e., "boat") and rate it on a pleasantness scale. Even though the question was essentially the same, people who were exposed to the second sentence rated "boat" to be significantly more pleasant (Whittlesea, 1993).

That result occurred because of *conceptual fluency*, a type of processing fluency related to how easily information comes to our mind (Alter & Oppenheimer, 2009). Generally, the faster a concept enters our mind, the more we tend to like it. Because the second sentence used particular words to prime the context, this heightened predictability caused the concept of "boat" to enter people's minds more easily, and that ease of processing produced a pleasant feeling that became misattributed to the word "boat."

Top-level marketers spend millions of dollars each year trying to take advantage of conceptual fluency. If we're deciding between two possible brands to purchase, we're likely to base our decision on how easily each brand comes to mind. When our opinion of two brands is the same, we're more likely to purchase the brand that comes to our mind more easily because that heightened conceptual fluency feels pleasant, and we mistakenly attribute that pleasantness to the brand (Nedungadi, 1990).

Marketers can take advantage of conceptual fluency and enhance the effectiveness of their advertisements by strategically positioning their ads in predictive contexts. For example, one study showed that consumers found a ketchup ad more favorable when the ad was presented after an ad for mayonnaise (Lee & Labroo, 2004). The mayonnaise ad primed consumers' schema for condiments, and when the ad for ketchup was presented afterward, the idea of ketchup came to their minds more easily. As a result of that heightened conceptual fluency, consumers developed a more positive attitude toward the ketchup advertisement.

How can you apply that technique in your own life? You can increase your chances of persuading someone to comply with a request by casually mentioning the topic of your request immediately prior to making it. Similar to the mayonnaise ad, the general topic will increase your target's conceptual fluency for your request, and as a result, your request will seem more appealing because it will come to your target's mind more easily. Your target will then misattribute that ease of processing with a desire to comply with your request.

Suppose that your favorite band is coming to town, and you want to persuade your friend to go to the concert with you next month. However, your friend doesn't really like the band, so you expect to encounter some resistance. In this situation, don't rush and hastily make your request now; instead, periodically bring up the idea of concerts in general for the next few days. With repeated exposure to that general topic, your friend will gradually develop a more positive attitude toward concerts in general, and he will be less resistant when you make your actual request. Also, because of conceptual fluency, the idea of accompanying you to the concert will enter his mind more easily when you eventually make your request, and he will mistakenly attribute that higher conceptual fluency with a desire to go to the concert.

**Use Any Repetitions.** In addition to influencing our perception and behavior, repeated exposures by themselves enhance our general mood. Monahan, Murphy, and Zajonc (2000) subliminally exposed a group of participants to 25 Chinese ideographs (symbols and characters used in Chinese writing), and they exposed each ideograph only once. However, with a different group of participants, they exposed only 5 Chinese ideographs, but they repeated the exposures five times. Remarkably, compared to participants who were subliminally exposed to 25 different ideographs, participants who were exposed to the repeated ideographs were in better moods after the exposures.

Afterward, the researchers asked each group to evaluate a few different stimuli, including the same ideographs, similar ideographs, and new unrelated polygons. Compared to participants who were shown one exposure of 25 ideographs, and compared to a control group that wasn't exposed to any ideographs, participants who were exposed to the repeated ideographs evaluated all other stimuli more positively because of their enhanced mood. The conclusion: merely experiencing any form of repeated event or exposure can enhance our feelings in general, which can then lead to greater positive feelings toward other stimuli that we encounter.

Have you noticed that all of the chapter titles in this book use a similar wording style? Every chapter title uses a sequence of three words (with an action verb as the first word), and this style is repeated for every chapter. Each time that you begin a new chapter and become exposed to that repeated wording style, your ease of processing that title can put you in a better mood, which can lead you to perceive the contents of that chapter more favorably.

**Create Greater Proximity.** If you were attending a college class in a large lecture hall with hundreds of students, would you remember every person from that class at the end of the semester? Probably not. But even if you don't remember a specific person, research shows that having been in the mere proximity of someone can create a favorable perception of that person.

Two researchers conducted a neat field experiment to test that claim (Moreland & Beach, 1992). The researchers asked four female students to be confederates in an experiment, and their job was to attend a predetermined number of classes in a psychology course (0, 5, 10, or 15 classes). Because they were instructed not to interact with other students, and because the classes were held in a large lecture hall, their presence was unnoticed by most students.

At the end of the semester, the researchers showed students a picture of each confederate that attended the class, and they asked the students to evaluate the four females. Despite possessing only vague memories, if any, for those confederates, students perceived the confederates to be more similar and attractive with the more classes they attended. When we're in the mere general vicinity of someone more often, that person is likely to find us more attractive!

*Sure,* you may be thinking, *people might prefer a photograph if they've been exposed to it before. Heck, people might even find someone more attractive if they were repeatedly exposed to that person. But is this effect strong enough to influence our actual behavior?*

Good question. Repeated exposures, even if they occur nonconsciously, can exert tremendous influence on our behavior as well. Remember the researchers who conducted the experiment with the geometric shapes? They conducted a follow-up experiment where they instructed people to read anonymous poems and collaborate with two other participants to make a unanimous decision regarding the gender of the anonymous poet. However, only one person was an actual participant in the experiment; the other two people were confederates hired by the researchers. They were instructed to disagree with each other, which would force the actual participant to then choose a side.

Before those discussions occurred, the genuine participants were repeatedly flashed with one of three pictures: a blank picture, a picture of Confederate A, or a picture of Confederate B (similar to the previous studies, these stimuli were flashed so quickly that participants failed to consciously notice them). The researchers wanted to examine how those nonconscious exposures would influence their interactions with the two confederates, and the results were startling.

Among participants who were flashed with a neutral blank picture, roughly 50 percent agreed with Confederate A, and 50 percent agreed with Confederate B, an expected even split. When participants were repeatedly flashed with a photograph of Confederate B prior to the discussion, 65 percent of participants agreed with Confederate B, and only 35 percent agreed with Confederate A. But when participants were instead flashed with a photograph of Confederate A, 71 percent of participants agreed with Confederate A, and only 29 percent agreed with Confederate B (Bornstein, Leone, & Galley, 1987). Repeated exposures not only influence our perception of a stimulus (e.g., someone's level of attractiveness), but repeated exposures can also influence our actual behavior, a very helpful notion when it comes to persuasion.

# CHAPTER 9

# Desensitize Negative Messages

When I originally wrote this book, I tried to illustrate the concept in this chapter by formatting the font in the previous chapter in a certain way. From section to section, I wanted to change a small aspect of the font until it reached a completely new style and size by the end of that chapter. In the original manuscript, the font began as 10 pt Georgia, but it ended as 11 pt Palatino Linotype (specifically, the font changed from 10 pt Georgia to 10.5 pt Cambria to 10.5 pt Palatino Linotype to 11 pt Palatino Linotype).

Though I wasn't able to incorporate those font changes due to the complexity of the formatting, editing, and publishing process, how the heck would that concept even relate to this chapter?

When you know that people will perceive your request to be unfavorable, you can sometimes habituate that request in small, incremental steps so that you can eventually integrate your entire message without their awareness. Because those font changes would have been so small, most readers would have remained completely oblivious to those changes. However, if they were to compare the beginning font with the end font, the difference would have been remarkable. This chapter will teach you exactly when and why many people become blind to certain changes and how you can present your message so that your target will become blind to negative aspects of your message.

This chapter also starts to border the ethical boundary, so I strongly urge you to exercise proper judgment when using these techniques. I wholeheartedly oppose anyone who tries to use these tactics for outcomes that aren't in other people's best interest. I even debated whether to include this chapter in the book, but there *are* many instances where camouflaging a negative feature can be in the best interest of other people (e.g., persuading your kids to enjoy eating vegetables or doing their homework).

## WHY DO SOME CHANGES GO UNNOTICED?

Why would readers be less apt to notice the font changes? By nature, we experience *change blindness*, an alarming inability to detect changes, especially when those changes are small and unexpected. This section will describe three facets of change blindness.

**Gradual Changes.** First, it's very difficult to detect changes that occur in small increments. There's a concept known as the *just noticeable difference* (or the *difference threshold*), which refers to the minimum amount of change that's needed in a stimulus in order for people to detect that change (Ono, 1967).

If you wanted, you could conduct a number of experiments to figure out the exact level of change that's needed for people to actually notice that a specific stimulus has been altered. Once you know the minimum percentage of change that triggers detection, you can make a change in your stimulus that's below that "just noticeable difference" so that your change remains undetected.

The previous wording may sound funky, so here's an example to illustrate. Suppose that you need to increase the price of a product that you sell, but you don't want that price increase to attract attention from consumers. You could conduct some experiments to determine the exact price point that people start to notice that increase in price, and you can then increase your price to a point below that "just noticeable difference" so that you minimize the number of people who notice your price increase.

If you're in a position where you can't conduct those experiments to figure out the exact level of difference that gets noticed, you can still intuitively take advantage of the difference threshold. Rather than make a large negative change to your message, you should "habituate" that message by making changes in small and gradual increments.

If I had immediately changed the font in the previous chapter from 10pt Georgia to 11pt Palatino Linotype, nearly everyone would notice because it's a very abrupt and prominent change. If those changes occurred in small and gradual increments, however, people would have been less apt to notice because those changes would have been more likely to fall below their difference threshold.

**Side-by-Side Comparisons.** Another facet of change blindness involves the ability to perform a side-by-side comparison of the original stimulus with the new stimulus. When people can perform a side-by-side comparison, any change will become much more readily noticed.

In the previous chapter, you would have been able to perform a side-by-side comparison of each section, so it would have been particularly important that the changes occur in very small increments. On the other hand, if each section had magically disappeared after you read it, the font changes would have become even more camouflaged because you would have no reference point to compare the new font.

Simons and Levin (1998) showed the alarming extent of our inability to detect change when we can't perform a side-by-side comparison. When a researcher asked a random passerby on the street for directions, two workers carrying a very large painting walked between them, and unbeknownst to the passerby, the researcher changed places with one of the workers behind the large painting. The goal was to find out how many people would continue the conversation with no idea that they were talking to a new person.

Take a guess at the percentage of people who were completely oblivious to the fact that they were talking to a new person. 5 percent? 10 percent? 15 percent? Nope. An astonishing *50 percent* of people failed to notice that they were talking to an entirely different person! Our ability to detect change becomes *dramatically* weakened when we can't compare the new stimulus to the original stimulus.

But as you'll learn next, there was another principle that caused people not to notice that large change.

**Expectations.** People didn't notice that they were talking to an entirely different person partly because they weren't expecting a change to occur.

Remember the exercise from the second chapter where people fail to notice the extra "a" in the phrase, "our brains can be a a mystery"? People expect to see that phrase without the extra "a," and so those expectations mold their perception to become oblivious to the discrepancy. Similarly, people *expected* to have a normal conversation with the researcher, and those expectations molded their perception so that they were oblivious to the striking change.

Let's look at an example that combines all three facets of change blindness. All three reasons discussed in this section—gradual changes, side-by-side comparisons, and expectations—can explain the mystery of the potato chip bag. Weren't potato chip bags much larger at one point? Indeed they were. Why did we fail to notice those reductions in size?

➤ First, marketers *gradually* reduced the size of the bag, and those changes were so small that most people failed to notice those changes.

➤ Second, unless people had a collection of potato chip bags in their home (which I'm assuming is a small percentage of people, but you never know . . .), people weren't able to perform a *side-by-side comparison* of the original bags with the newer bags.

➤ Third, marketers changed the size to avoid changing something that people *do* typically notice: prices. Although we're constantly on guard about potential price increases, we don't typically "expect" the size of potato chip bags to change, so marketers cleverly took advantage of our diverted attention.

Now that you know the reasons when and why we fail to notice changes, the next section will teach you how to apply this principle so that people will fail to notice negative aspects about your message.

# PERSUASION STRATEGY: DESENSITIZE NEGATIVE MESSAGES

This section will explain how to use change blindness to influence your target to accept a message or comply with a request, even if he finds it unfavorable (e.g., parents persuading their child to eat vegetables).

**Systematic Desensitization.** In certain situations where your target will find your message unfavorable, you can habituate that message through *systematic desensitization*. Most commonly used as a form of therapy, systematic desensitization helps people overcome phobias by gradually exposing them to more and more anxiety-arousing stimuli.

Consider "Little Peter," a 2-year-old boy who was terrified of rabbits (Jones, 1924). To help him overcome his fear, a researcher gave him candy (a stimulus that produced a favorable response) while placing a rabbit in the far side of the room. Because the rabbit was still far away, the positive response from the candy overpowered the anxiety produced from the rabbit. That process was repeated every day for the following two months, and each time, the researcher brought the rabbit *slightly* closer to Peter. By the end of the two months, Peter had become so desensitized to the rabbit's presence that his fear had completely vanished.

Do you have a phobia that you want to overcome? Systematic desensitization works on adults as well. Researchers in one case study explained how they helped a woman overcome her severe phobia of spiders by exposing her to increasingly stressful spider-related stimuli (Carlin, Hoffman, & Weghorst, 1997). Over the span of a few months, they started by simply talking about spiders and then gradually increased to exposing photographs of spiders, fake toy spiders, and even spiders in virtual reality. By the end of the therapy, the researchers had resolved the woman's incapacitating fear of spiders.

*That's great, Nick. But how does that relate to persuasion?* I'm glad you asked. Remember how I mentioned the example of parents persuading their kids to enjoy vegetables? If your kids really enjoy a particular meal—a meal that could easily be tweaked to incorporate vegetables— you could add a miniscule amount of vegetables the next time you cook that meal. With only a miniscule amount, your kids might eat the meal without asking any questions.

But each additional time that you cook that meal, you can *slightly* increase the amount of vegetables. Because your kids won't be able to perform a side-by-side comparison with the last meal, they'll be unlikely to notice that you put more vegetables in that meal. They might even think back and remember that they ate that same meal with a miniscule amount of something unknown, and because they still enjoyed it, they're more likely to remain consistent with that original attitude by continuing to eat that meal with the slightly increased vegetable content.

You can continue that same process for months until your children finally notice *something*. But once they realize that they've been enjoying the meal for months *with* the vegetables, research suggests that they'll be more likely to want to continue eating it with the vegetables (Lee, Frederick, & Ariely, 2006).

To summarize, if you want people to develop a favorable (or even neutral) attitude toward something that you know they will find unfavorable, you can "desensitize" your message by gradually habituating that message. This technique will be even more effective if: (1) the changes occur in small and gradual increments, (2) your target can't perform a side-by-side comparison, (3) your target isn't expecting any changes to occur, or (4) you combine the unfavorable stimulus with a pleasant stimulus (e.g., combining the candy with the rabbit, combining the yummy meal with the addition of vegetables).

## A MIND READER'S PERSPECTIVE: DESENSITIZING SLEIGHT OF HAND

Before I changed my official title to "mind reader," I performed as a "magician" for over five years. During that time, I became exposed to countless sleight of hand techniques that magicians use to avoid being detected. One common technique that magicians use to disguise their sleight of hand involves desensitizing their audience's perception.

Put yourself in my shoes. You're performing a mind reading show on stage, and you just tried to nonconsciously prime a particular thought in someone's mind, but due to some clever and subtle questions, you discover that your attempt at priming failed. But as the stubborn mind reader you are, you don't want to admit defeat. You want to figure out a way to make it seem like you still knew what that person was thinking.

You try to recover by resorting to Plan B. The new goal is to ask the person to name their thought out loud, while you undetectably write whatever they say on a piece of paper inside your pocket. If you can write that person's thought undetected, you can use sleight of hand to switch the paper inside your pocket for a folded piece of paper that you're holding in front of the audience. This switch can make it seem like you predicted that person's thought from the very beginning, and you'll still have a miracle in your hands (so to speak).

There's a problem, however. If you just randomly stick your hand in your pocket, you'll probably attract the audience's attention, which would defeat Plan B. How can you disguise that action? You can desensitize the audience to the placement of your hand in your pocket by frequently putting your hand in your pocket throughout the show. This frequent positioning would desensitize the audience to the idea of your hand in your pocket, and they'll be less likely to notice your hand in your pocket when you need to write the prediction. It takes a lot of practice to pull off undetectably, but that's the trouble that many mind readers go through.

This type of demonstration would be much easier if you were doing it over a webcam because you wouldn't even need to worry about a pocket; you could just write on the desk in front of you. In fact, with some proper showmanship, you could use this demonstration to freak people out via webcam and end up creating a viral video (hint: my video "Chat Roulette Mind Reading—Part 1").

# REAL WORLD APPLICATION:
# THE FAMILY VACATION (PART 2)

Remember the family vacation to Disneyland? Your budget-concerned husband is on the fence about taking the trip, but you decide to put the odds in your favor by habituating your request.

You leverage repeated exposures by "forgetting" to leave travel brochures, postcards, and other travel-related advertisements throughout the house. These advertisements will repeatedly expose your husband to the idea of taking a vacation, which will make him find the idea of travel more appealing. These tactics will be even more effective because, as you learned, nonconscious exposures are more powerful than conscious exposures. If your husband doesn't consciously pay attention to these subtle advertisements, his attitude toward the vacation will be further enhanced through the mere exposure effect.

Those repeated exposures will also enhance your husband's conceptual fluency for travel. When you bring up the idea again, he will be able to picture himself on vacation more easily because of those exposures, and he will misattribute that ease to a genuine desire to go on vacation.

After a week or two of letting these travel ads lie around the house, you finally ask him about his stance on the vacation. This time, your husband is somewhat more open to the idea, but he says that he still needs time to think about it. Ugh. You failed again to extract his compliance, but don't fret. Luckily, there are still many more tactics to be covered, so we'll revisit this scenario later in the book.

# STEP 5

# Optimize Your Message

| | | | |
|---|---|---|---|
| **Before the Request** | *Step 1:* | **M** | Mold Their Perception |
| | *Step 2:* | **E** | Elicit Congruent Attitudes |
| | *Step 3:* | **T** | Trigger Social Pressure |
| | *Step 4:* | **H** | Habituate Your Message |
| **During the Request** | ***Step 5:*** | **O** | **Optimize Your Message** |
| | *Step 6:* | **D** | Drive Their Momentum |
| **After the Request** | *Step 7:* | **S** | Sustain Their Compliance |

## OVERVIEW:
## OPTIMIZE YOUR MESSAGE

Look at that! We *finally* made it to the request. Let's do a quick recap to summarize the four steps that brought you here:

➤ First, you molded your target's mindset though priming, anchoring, and expectations, which helped you trigger a more favorable perception.

➤ Second, you changed your target's body language and behavior to reflect someone who would comply with your request, which helped you extract a congruent attitude. As a result, your target has become much more likely to comply with your request to maintain consistency with that new attitude.

➤ Third, you emphasized social norms and built greater rapport so that you could exert additional pressure on your target.

➤ Fourth, you used repeated exposures and desensitization to habituate your target to your message. With heightened familiarity toward the topic of your request, your target has become even more likely to comply with it.

This next step in METHODS will teach you the proper way to present your message or request. Specifically, you'll learn how people typically evaluate messages depending on the circumstances, and you'll learn how to properly tweak your message so that it complements how your target will evaluate your message.

# CHAPTER 10

# Alter Their Evaluation

You trudge to work one morning overwhelmed with tiredness. You spent the entire night perfecting a monthly report so that you could impress your new boss. But your hard work paid off. You're overjoyed with the final outcome, and you're confident that your boss will recognize and appreciate your hard work.

You enter the building, walk directly to your boss's office, and drop the report on her desk with a huge smile on your face. However, to your chagrin, your boss picks up the report, lightly flips through the pages, and hands the report back to you with a simple, "Thanks, it looks good." Mortified that you spent the entire night working on a report that your boss merely glanced at for a few seconds, you trudge back to your desk and fight off the urge to fall asleep.

A few weeks later, the next monthly report is due. But you won't make the same mistake again. Why bother putting forth the extra effort when your boss is only going to glance at it for a few seconds? This time, you only spend a half hour creating a semi-decent report so that you can leave work on time.

Next morning you walk into your boss's office, drop the report on her desk, and to your mortification, your boss wants to critically evaluate it. She tells you that she'll look through it and discuss it with you later that afternoon. You walk out of her office and trudge back to your desk with a huge knot in your stomach because you know that your competence will be judged in a poor light.

Whether it's beneficial or harmful for your situation, people evaluate information differently depending on the circumstances. This chapter will teach you the two most basic ways that people evaluate messages and how you can trigger the most favorable type of evaluation for your situation.

## THE TWO WAYS THAT PEOPLE EVALUATE MESSAGES

There are two basic ways in which we evaluate information: we use either systematic or heuristic processing (Chaiken, 1980).

**Systematic Processing.** When the boss analyzed and scrutinized the report, she was using *systematic processing*, an effortful evaluation that involves critically analyzing information. When we use systematic processing (also known as the *central route to persuasion*), we're more influenced by the underlying arguments and content of information. Would you ever:

➤ Spontaneously buy a house?
➤ Throw a dart at a map to decide your next vacation?
➤ Choose your brain surgeon based on his attractiveness?

Of course not. In those circumstances, you would do your homework and critically evaluate all of the details involved so that you can make a proper decision. But, as you'll see next, we don't always do that.

**Heuristic Processing.** When the boss judged the monthly report by lightly flipping through the pages, she was using *heuristic processing*, a simple-minded evaluation that relies on quick decision rules. When we use heuristic processing (also known as the *peripheral route to persuasion*), we're more influenced by simple, irrelevant, and "peripheral" cues, such as:

➤ The sheer amount of information or support
➤ The aesthetics of a message
➤ The person presenting the message (e.g., his likability, attractiveness, perceived expertise, etc.)

Those peripheral cues don't necessarily relate to the strength of a message, yet people often use those "heuristics" to make quick judgments about the overall content of information.

Now that you understand the difference between systematic and heuristic processing, the next section explains the two factors that determine which type of evaluation will generally be used in a given situation.

## TWO FACTORS THAT DETERMINE
## HOW YOUR MESSAGE WILL BE EVALUATED

Two main researchers in the field of persuasion, Richard Petty and John Cacioppo (1986), developed the *elaboration-likelihood model* to describe the factors that determine how a message will be evaluated (whether systematically or heuristically). This section will describe the two main factors that they found in their research: motivation and ability to evaluate.

**Motivation.** The first factor is someone's motivation to evaluate your message. When your target's motivation is high, your message will be evaluated using systematic processing; when your target's motivation is low, your message will be evaluated using heuristic processing.

It might seem like an obvious conclusion, but what exactly determines someone's motivation? Perhaps the most important aspect is the perceived importance of your message. Your target will be more motivated to critically evaluate your message when they view that information as important to understand.

Consider this book as an example. When people read the sales description for *Methods of Persuasion*, which type of evaluation—systematic or heuristic—do you think most people use? Though I'd like to think that people carefully evaluate the description of my book, with all else being equal, people are likely to base their purchase decision on a simple-minded evaluation. Why? Most people don't view a book purchase to be a life-altering event; there are very few significant outcomes for their compliance (or lack thereof). Rather than carefully read the description or seek information elsewhere on the web, they're likely to base their decision on irrelevant heuristics, such as the number of positive reviews or my perceived popularity.

Some of you might be questioning the previous claim because you can remember instances where you *did* decide to purchase a book based on a careful evaluation of the description. Though it might seem like a discrepancy, you need to remember that circumstances (e.g., a book purchase) don't determine how your message is evaluated; it's the level of motivation in someone. It could be the most trivial situation possible, but if someone has high motivation to evaluate the relevant information, then he will use systematic processing.

**Ability.** Your target's ability to evaluate is the second factor that determines how your message is evaluated. This section explains two aspects of someone's ability: their intellectual capacity and opportunity to evaluate.

*Intellectual Capacity.* One aspect of people's ability to evaluate is their intellectual capacity, which is different than general intelligence. If I was listening to a speech on supersymmetric quantum mechanics, I would have absolutely no idea what the speaker was talking about. Does that mean I'm stupid? No. It simply means that I don't know enough about that specific topic. In this situation, you bet that I would rely on peripheral cues (e.g., the speaker's confidence or presentation style) to judge the accuracy and strength of the speech's content. How else could I evaluate the speech if I don't understand the actual message? In this situation, my intellectual capacity would be too low to use systematic processing to evaluate the arguments, and so I'm forced to rely on peripheral cues to evaluate the speech.

*Opportunity.* The second aspect of your target's ability to evaluate is related to external constraints. If your target is lacking time or if there are many distractions, then she will speed up her evaluation by relying on peripheral cues, such as your likability and attractiveness. Perhaps your boss was in a rush when she evaluated the first monthly report, so she simply judged the content of the report based on your high level of confidence. Using that simple yet irrelevant cue to judge the report was much faster than digesting the actual content in the report. But perhaps your boss's schedule was less hectic for the second monthly report, and so she had a greater opportunity to evaluate it.

## PERSUASION STRATEGY: ALTER THEIR EVALUATION

The previous section explained that motivation and ability to evaluate are the two factors that determine how people evaluate messages. When your target's motivation and ability are *low*, your target will rely on peripheral cues to judge your message (e.g., number of arguments, aesthetics, their perception of you). When your target's motivation and ability are *high*, your target will effortfully evaluate your message and judge it based on the strength of your arguments.

This step in METHODS will teach you two overall strategies to apply that knowledge toward successful persuasion; you can either:

1.  Alter your target's motivation or ability to ensure that your message is evaluated in the most favorable manner (explained in this chapter), or you can . . .
2.  Use your knowledge of the previous factors to predict how your target will evaluate your message so that you can tweak your message accordingly (explained in the next chapter).

In this first persuasion strategy, you alter the factors that you learned in the previous section to ensure that your target evaluates your message in the most favorable manner (whether that evaluation is systematic or heuristic processing).

If there are strong reasons why your target should comply with your request, you should ensure that your target evaluates those reasons using systematic processing. On the other hand, if you think that the odds are stacked against you because your arguments are very weak, then don't worry . . . you're not completely screwed yet! If you get your target to evaluate your message using heuristic processing, you can cause her to brush over your weak arguments and judge your message based on other factors that are irrelevant to your actual message.

## HOW TO ELICIT SYSTEMATIC PROCESSING

There are many ways to alter your target's motivation and ability so that they use systematic processing. This section will describe two example strategies: grab someone's attention and increase the relevance of your message.

**Grab Their Attention.** People consistently function on autopilot. Do you ever hang up on telemarketers without actually listening to what they're selling? When you present a request to people, they will often feel a natural reflex to immediately reject your request because that's the reaction to which they've become accustomed.

In order to prevent that mindless refusal and elicit an effortful evaluation of your message, you need to first successfully grab their attention. How? Here are three simple techniques that you can use to capture someone's attention:

➤ *Give 'Em Caffeine.* Wait, caffeine? What the heck are you supposed to do—ask your target if she wants a cup of coffee before you make your request? Well, why not? It couldn't hurt. In fact, research shows that caffeine significantly enhances systematic processing. In one study, researchers exposed students to arguments about voluntary euthanasia, a message that all of the students opposed. However, students who consumed a caffeinated drink were significantly more persuaded by the arguments compared to students who didn't consume a caffeinated drink (Martin et al., 2007). If the circumstances are suitable, you can ensure that your message is evaluated in a more effortful manner by offering your target a caffeinated drink (perhaps you take your client to a coffee shop to discuss your business proposal).

➤ *Enhance Message Aesthetics.* If a caffeinated drink is out of the question, research also shows that enhancing the aesthetics of your message can also grab people's attention so that they pay more attention to your underlying arguments (MacInnis, Moorman, & Jaworski, 1991). You've probably been watching television when a visually stunning commercial appears and grabs your attention. Once it grabs your attention, you think that it might contain an important or compelling message, and so you pay more attention to that commercial.

➤ *Pique Technique.* One final technique to capture your target's attention is the *pique technique*. Rather than plainly state an ordinary request, you can present your request in an odd manner to snap your target out of her autopilot state of mind. To test that claim, research assistants disguised themselves as beggars and asked people on the street for either 17 cents, a quarter, 37 cents, or "any change." What's interesting is that the "beggars" received more money when the request was unusual (17 cents and 37 cents) because people on the street were yanked from autopilot, and they were forced to evaluate the odd request instead of mindlessly refusing it (Santos, Leve, & Pratkanis, 1994).

**Increase Personal Relevance.** In addition to grabbing your target's attention, you can also trigger a more effortful evaluation of your message by enhancing its perceived relevance to your target. If your target believes that your message will affect him—either positively or negatively—then he'll be more motivated to pay attention to your message (Petty & Cacioppo, 1990).

One basic technique involves describing the consequences of your message, especially in a vivid manner. For example, commercials about driver safety are much more effective when they show vivid images of bloody victims, rather than images of test dummies (Rogers & Mewborn, 1976).

But there are others techniques besides describing the consequences. Here are three other specific techniques that you can use to enhance the perceived relevance of your message:

➤ *Use 2nd Person Pronouns.* Research in advertising shows that using the word "you" in a message can dramatically increase the persuasiveness of an advertisement. For instance, when people evaluated an advertisement for a calculator, they developed a significantly more favorable attitude toward the calculator when the researchers used 2nd person pronouns (e.g., "You know that calculator technology . . . ," "You may remember . . .") compared to neutral statements (e.g., "If a mistake was made . . .") (Burnkrant & Unnava, 1995).

➤ *Tell a Story.* Do you ever wonder why television advertisers try to communicate their product benefits by depicting a story or narrative with characters/actors? Why not simply describe the benefits of their product instead? When television viewers watch a narrative commercial, they empathize with the characters (especially if they view them to be similar), and viewers start to picture themselves using the product in their own life (Deighton, Romer, & McQueen, 1989).

➤ *Ask Rhetorical Questions.* Have you wondered why I ask so many rhetorical questions throughout this book, such as this rhetorical question that you're reading right now? I use a lot of rhetorical questions because they spark greater personal relevance. When students were exposed to a message arguing for a comprehensive exam for seniors, they were more persuaded when the arguments were presented in a rhetorical manner (e.g., "Don't you agree that . . . ," "Isn't it true that . . .") because those questions subtly influenced students to relate the arguments to their own life (Petty, Cacioppo, & Heesacker, 1981).

Now that you understand how to increase someone's motivation and ability to extract an effortful evaluation of your message, the next section will explain how to decrease someone's motivation and ability so that you can extract a simple-minded evaluation of your message.

## HOW TO ELICIT HEURISTIC PROCESSING

If the arguments in your message are fairly weak, you'll want to elicit a greater reliance on heuristic processing. How can you do that? It might be easier than you think. If you picture your target as a computer program, her default setting is heuristic processing. In other words, if you don't do anything to increase her motivation or ability, she will typically default to evaluating your request in a simple-minded manner. But if you want to further enhance this reliance, you can implement a few techniques to subtly dissuade your target from relying on systematic processing. Three example strategies include increasing the complexity of your message, enhancing their mood, and sparking their arousal.

**Increase Message Complexity.** When it comes to persuasion, we're usually told to make our message as clear as possible. Surprisingly, however, that's not always the best strategy. There are some situations where increasing the complexity of your message can actually help you persuade your target. That notion can help explain why people are more likely to buy gourmet cheese if an advertisement describes it in a difficult-to-read font, compared to an easy-to-read font (Pocheptsova, Labroo, & Dhar, 2010).

The explanation to that odd finding can be found in processing fluency. Remember how people misattribute their evaluation of information to the ease and speed with which they process that information? I explained how people who list 12 instances of their assertiveness perceive themselves to be less assertive (compared to people who list 6 instances) because they misattributed their difficulty in generating examples to a low level of assertiveness.

People make similar misattributions when they view advertisements for unique products, such as gourmet cheese. People were more likely to purchase a gourmet cheese when an advertisement described it in a difficult-to-read font because people misattributed the difficulty in processing to the uniqueness of the cheese, a perception that made it seem more appealing. When the advertisement was depicting an everyday cheese, that effect disappeared; people were more likely to purchase an everyday cheese when the advertisement described it in an easy-to-read font because that ease of processing generated feelings of familiarity.

Processing fluency and message complexity can also enhance the perception of other stimuli. Consider a research study that involved a description of an online coaching service that helps students apply to graduate school. Students perceived that service to be more valuable and they were more willing to pay for a one-year subscription when the coaching service was presented using a light blue font with a white background (a difficult-to-read display) compared to when it was presented using a black font with a white background (an easy-to-read display). Students developed a more favorable evaluation of the coaching service when it was presented in a difficult-to-read format because they misattributed their difficulty in processing to the difficulty in applying to graduate school, a perception that sparked a greater need for the coaching service (Thompson & Chandon Ince, 2013).

If you want your target to perceive your product to be unique or your service to be difficult, you can create this perception by increasing the perceived complexity of your message (e.g., using a difficult-to-read font). Presenting your message in a difficult-to-process format can decrease your target's motivation and ability to evaluate your message, which can make them more likely to rely on other factors, such as processing fluency, to make their evaluation. If you can maintain an aesthetically pleasing message while decreasing processing fluency, you can cause people to perceive your product to be more unique or your service to be more difficult (thereby leading to a higher perceived value).

**Enhance Their Mood.** Another factor that can decrease people's motivation to evaluate a message is their mood. Generally, people who are in happy moods are less likely to critically evaluate a message (Bless et al., 1990).

When we're in positive moods, we often develop a sense of naïve optimism. For example, one factor that perpetuates a financial bubble is irrational exuberance, a term coined by Alan Greenspan, former chairman of the Federal Reserve. During the "dot-com bubble" in the late 90s, stock prices of Internet companies skyrocketed over several years, rising to a point where the underlying financials of those companies didn't support the overinflated stock prices. As stock prices continued to soar, people developed a sense of naïve optimism and irrational exuberance. The positive emotions they experienced from their large gains led to a false assumption that stock prices would continue to rise, a perception that blinded them to the imminent burst of the bubble and the resulting depletion of their bank accounts.

Unlike positive moods, negative moods lead to a greater sense of skepticism. When people are in negative moods, they subtly assume that something must be wrong with a message, and that uncertainty causes them to analyze messages with a fine-toothed comb. Research has even confirmed that people in happy moods are influenced by both strong and weak arguments, whereas people in neutral or negative moods are only influenced by strong arguments (Mackie & Worth, 1991).

If you want your message to be evaluated simple-mindedly, or if your request is somewhat risky in nature, you should first brighten your target's mood so that he develops a greater sense of optimism and a greater likelihood of complying with your request.

**Spark Their Arousal.** Get your mind out of the gutter. This "arousal" is different than the sexual type of arousal, and this arousal can spark heuristic processing.

To understand this type of arousal, you first need to understand another concept. As humans, we think that we possess a solid grasp of our own emotions and feelings, and we tend to believe that all types of emotions—sadness, excitement, fear, etc.—produce different sensations and feelings within us. What's surprising is that many of those emotions produce the same exact physiological response.

If they produce the same biological reactions, why do they feel so different? Stanley Schachter and Jerome Singer (1962) proposed their *two-factor theory of emotion* to explain that we interpret emotional responses in two steps. First, we experience some general physiological arousal in response to a stimulus, and this "arousal" is usually characterized by a rapid heartbeat, heavy breathing, sweaty palms, and other symptoms that are related to higher adrenaline. Second, after experiencing that state of arousal, we then look to the situation to interpret that state of arousal, and we label that arousal with the emotion that seems most fitting.

Consider two scenarios. In the first scenario, you're walking down an alley late at night in a dangerous city, and out of the darkness appears a man with a gun asking for all of your money. In this situation, nearly all humans would feel a very powerful state of arousal, characterized by a rapid heartbeat, heavy breathing, sweaty palms, etc.

In the other scenario, suppose that you bought a lottery ticket, and you're sitting at home waiting for the numbers to be called. The television host appears, announces the numbers, and you realize that all of your numbers match. You just won $50 million dollars. How would your body react? You'd probably experience a rapid heartbeat, heavy breathing, sweaty palms, and virtually all other symptoms that occurred when you were robbed.

Although getting robbed and winning the lottery are two very different scenarios, they produce very similar bodily reactions. Schachter and Singer proposed that those emotions feel very different (despite the same biological reactions) because we look to our environment and circumstances to label that arousal. In the first situation, we recognize that we're being robbed, and so we label our arousal as fear. But in the second situation, we realize that we won a huge chunk of money, and so we label our arousal as excitement. Next time that you're doing something that generates fear (e.g., public speaking), you could help ease your anxiety by giving your arousal a different label, such as excitement.

But in addition to persuading yourself, how can arousal help you persuade other people? Research shows that activating arousal can be beneficial because it activates heuristic processing. For example, people who were induced into a state of arousal via exercise were more influenced by a celebrity endorser (Sanbonmatsu & Kardes, 1988). If you need to ask your friend for a favor, you might be able to increase your chances of persuading her if you wait for your weekly trip to the gym to spring that request on her. Keep this concept of arousal in the back of your mind because the final chapter will revisit it and explain a few other applications and uses of arousal for persuasion.

But now that you know how to elicit a favorable evaluation of your request, the next chapter will discuss a reciprocal strategy: tweaking your message to suit a particular evaluation.

# CHAPTER 11

# Tweak Your Message

The previous chapter described how you can alter people's motivation and ability to evaluate so that you can extract the most favorable type of evaluation for your message. Albeit an effective strategy, you'll encounter instances where you won't be able to change people's evaluation. Are you out of luck? Nope. You just need to predict which type of evaluation they *will* use (by judging their motivation and ability), and you can tweak your message to better suit that evaluation. This chapter will jump straight to the persuasion strategies because the previous chapter already explained the relevant psychology.

## PERSUASION STRATEGY: TWEAK YOUR MESSAGE

Here's the overall strategy: if you know that your target will use systematic processing, you should focus on enhancing the strength of your arguments; if you know that your target will use heuristic processing, you should focus more attention on enhancing the peripheral aspects of your message. The persuasion strategies in this section will teach you some practical techniques to accomplish each of those goals.

### *HOW TO TWEAK YOUR MESSAGE FOR SYSTEMATIC PROCESSING*

Unlike heuristic processing, which can be enhanced through many different aspects, systematic processing can only be enhanced through one main aspect: the strength of your message.

If you predict that your target will have high motivation and ability to evaluate your message, then you need to focus on building stronger supporting arguments. If you're in a situation where you can't improve the strength of your reasons, then you have two options. First, you can rely on the persuasion strategy in the previous chapter and decrease your target's motivation and ability (e.g., decrease personal relevance, don't grab their attention, etc.) so that they evaluate your message in a more simple-minded manner. The other option, however, is to enhance the *perceived* strength of your arguments. Luckily, there are a few very simple adjustments you can make to most messages that will enhance the perceived strength of the content. This section describes two techniques: using two-sided arguments and sequencing arguments properly.

**Present Two-Sided Arguments.** Counterintuitive to our current beliefs, presenting a little bit of negative information about your message can actually benefit you. Research shows that two-sided arguments (arguments that present both positive and negative aspects of a message) can produce favorable changes in attitude and behavior (Rucker, Petty, & Briñol, 2008).

When a message contains only positive support, people tend to believe that the message is purposely excluding information, which causes them to be skeptical toward that message. On the other hand, when a message contains a small amount of negative information, people develop stronger attitudes because they believe that the information is more complete. When the situation is suitable, you should include a small amount of negative information in your message (as well as arguments to address and counter that negative information) because people will assume that you've considered both sides of the topic, and as a result, you'll be able to persuade them more easily.

**Properly Sequence Your Arguments.** In some situations, you'll be providing a number of arguments to support your message (e.g., a school essay, a business proposal). To maximize the appeal of your message, you need to properly sequence those arguments.

Remember the primacy effect from the second chapter? It explained how information presented earlier in a sequence can influence how people perceive the rest of the information in that sequence. Similarly, there's another powerful effect called the *recency effect*, which causes people to remember the final pieces of information in a sequence more easily than other pieces of information in that same sequence (Murdock, 1962). Let's examine how you can use the primacy and recency effect to properly sequence arguments and enhance the strength of your message.

*Position Strong Arguments First and Last.* Whether you're writing a school essay, crafting a business proposal, or simply listing the reasons why your target should comply with your request, you should position your most compelling arguments first and last in your sequence. Those arguments will carry more weight in those positions due to the primacy and recency effect.

This advice also applies in situations where your performance will be judged against other people (e.g., talent show, job interview). You can enhance your perceived performance and become more memorable by choosing the first or last position in the line-up. Those positions are also favorable because they take advantage of conceptual fluency: when the judges are choosing the winner at the end, the first and last positions will come to their mind more easily, making the judges prone to misattributing that ease of remembering to a superior performance. If they can easily remember your performance, they will mistakenly jump to the conclusion that your performance was better than the others.

Suppose that you're scheduling an interview for a job and you learn that the human resources person will be interviewing candidates throughout the course of the day. To increase your chances of getting the job, you should schedule the interview early in the morning (hopefully before all other candidates) or late in the afternoon (hopefully after all other candidates). Because those positions are more easily remembered, you stand a better chance of getting the job by remaining at the top of their awareness when they pick the winning candidate.

Are the first and last positions equal, or is one position more powerful than the other? If you're a dedicated persuasion-ist and you want to take this sequencing strategy a step further, you should put your most compelling argument last when your target must decide immediately. Why? Because that argument will be in your target's working memory when he makes the looming decision (Miller & Campbell, 1959). On the other hand, if your target will be waiting before deciding, then you should put your most compelling argument first because the primacy effect is more powerful in the long run.

In the previous job scenario, you should schedule your interview for late in the afternoon if you know that the company will be making a hiring decision very soon (because the recency effect is stronger in the short-term). But if you know that the company will not make a decision for a while, then you should schedule your interview as early as possible because the primacy effect becomes dominant over time.

*Position Weak Arguments in the Middle.* Remember how it can be beneficial to include a small amount of negative information in your message? If you follow that advice, you should position that negative information in the middle of your sequence of arguments. Not only will that position still lead to the benefit of giving your message a more comprehensive appearance, but that negative information will then be more likely to fly under your target's radar.

You should *never* position negative information or weak arguments first because of a potentially harmful principle known as the *inoculation effect* (McGuire, 1964). When a doctor gives you a shot (i.e., an inoculation), you typically receive a small dosage of the infection or disease so that your body can build an immunity to protect against it. The same concept applies to persuasion. If we're first exposed to a weak argument, we resist that weak argument and develop greater resistance toward future arguments, even if those future arguments are stronger. Once we successfully resist an initial attempt at persuasion, we develop persuasion "antibodies" that help us resist future attacks more easily. You should always strive to make a good first impression because, once an impression has been formed, it becomes increasingly more difficult to change it.

## HOW TO TWEAK YOUR MESSAGE FOR HEURISTIC PROCESSING

There are an endless number of heuristics that people use to evaluate messages, but most of them relate to either you or your message. This section describes a few of those heuristics and how you can enhance them.

**Their Perception of You.** You're in a bar one night, and the drunkest man in the bar shouts and screams that the end of the world is approaching. Though an objectively scary claim, it probably wouldn't faze you in the slightest bit. But suppose that, instead of a drunkard at the bar, a renowned scientist appears on television and claims that the end of the world is approaching. It's the same exact claim, yet you're now significantly more likely to wet yourself from fear.

People's perception of a communicator can be a powerful heuristic that they use to immediately accept or reject a particular message. This section will explain two powerful aspects of that heuristic: perceived authority and attractiveness.

*Authority.* If somebody told you to give an extremely powerful electric shock to an innocent bystander, would you do it? What if the person instructing you was wearing a lab coat? Would that make a difference? In one of the most groundbreaking and controversial experiments in the history of psychology, Stanley Milgram found that it makes a tremendous difference (Milgram, 1963).

In that experiment, two participants entered a room and waited for an experimenter. One person was a genuine participant, and unbeknownst to him, the other participant was a confederate hired by the experimenter.

After the two "participants" greeted each other, the experimenter entered the room and explained that the experiment was examining learning. He told participants that each of them would be randomly assigned to one of two roles: one participant would be given the role of "teacher," and the other participant would be given the role of "learner." The supposed randomness was actually fixed; the confederate was always the learner, and the true participant was always the teacher.

The experimenter then explained that the study was examining electric shock on learning, and the true participant watched the experimenter tightly strap the confederate into a scary-looking chair that would deliver the electric shocks. The participant's role as "teacher" involved asking the "learner" a series of memory questions from a separate room. Each time that the confederate answered a question incorrectly, the participant was required to push a button that delivered an electric shock to him in the other room. The levels of shock ranged from 15 volts to a near-lethal 450 volts, increasing in 15-volt increments. With each incorrect answer, the participant was instructed to deliver a higher incremental shock.

Unbeknownst to the participant, the confederate in the other room wasn't actually receiving shocks. Instead, the experiment was examining the extent to which people would obey the experimenter's request to deliver the shocks (despite the confederate's grunts that gradually escalated to agonizing screams of severe heart pain).

If at any point the participant asked the experimenter if he could stop delivering the shocks, the experimenter would give four prods in the following order:

1. Please continue.
2. The experiment requires that you continue.
3. It is absolutely essential that you continue.
4. You have no other choice but to continue.

If the participant persisted on stopping even after those four prods, then the experiment was terminated.

The results of the study were "shocking." A staggering 65 percent of people administered the highest level of voltage (which participants were informed was near lethal). Even when they heard severe screams of pain, the majority of people still gave a powerful electric shock that could have killed another person.

This experiment has been conducted across the globe, and although the percentages vary depending on the culture, the results are generally consistent: humans are psychologically compelled to obey authority figures to a very large and frightening extent. Even ordinary and moral citizens will perform unthinkable acts if instructed by a higher authority.

How does that relate to persuasion? Much like our tendency to blindly follow authority, we also blindly trust experts in a particular field. When an expert makes a certain claim, rather than use systematic processing to critically evaluate that information, we often blindly trust the accuracy of that information merely because it came from an "expert." For example, when students read a speech about acid rain, students who were told that the speech was written by an environmental studies major were more persuaded by the speech than students who were told that the speech was written by a mathematics major, even though the speech was exactly the same (Mackie & Worth, 1991).

If you're not yet considered an expert, you can still use experts' testimony to support your claims. With *Methods of Persuasion* being my first book, my perceived authority in this area is pretty low. Rather than try to convince you of my authority and knowledge, I tried to overcome that hurdle by heavily citing research to support my claims. In fact, I almost used footnotes for the citations, but I deliberately chose to include citations within the text to reinforce that these strategies are grounded in credible research.

*Attractiveness.* In a perfect world, attractiveness shouldn't affect your persuasion. But wait—we're *not* living in a perfect world. Does attractiveness matter? Yes it does. Unfortunately, it matters to a scary extent. Take a look at some disturbing findings:

➢ Attractive criminals receive more lenient sentences (Sigall & Ostrove, 1975).

➢ Attractive infants receive more attention and caretaking (Glocker et al., 2009).

➢ Attractive men receive higher starting salaries, and attractive women earn more money later in their career (Frieze, Olson, & Russell, 1991).

Despite those positive benefits, are attractive people inherently "better" than other people? Many researchers have examined that question, but most have failed to produce evidence to support that claim. One of the only reliable traits where attractive people have a genuine advantage over other people is mating success (Rhodes et al., 2005).

All of the other benefits from physical attractiveness have emerged through psychological factors. Attractive people have a significant advantage because other people unknowingly act more favorably toward them. For example, when male students in one study were led to believe that they were speaking with an attractive female over the phone, not only did they develop a more favorable impression of the female's personality, but the women on the other line, in turn, developed a favorable impression of the male's personality (Snyder, Decker Tanke, & Berscheid, 1977).

Despite all of those alarming claims about attractiveness, there *are* techniques that you can use to enhance your perceived attractiveness. Two techniques that were discussed earlier include familiarity and similarity (Moreland & Beach, 1992; Montoya, Horton, & Kirchner, 2008). You can enhance your perceived attractiveness by: (1) being in the general vicinity of someone more often and, (2) revealing any type of similarity that you might share with that person.

But there's another, more powerful technique that you can use. The final chapter will expand on this concept and explain another powerful way to enhance your perceived attractiveness (and why you'd have greater success in meeting a potential romantic partner at a gym).

**Their Perception of Your Message.** Heuristics can be found not only in the source of a message (e.g., a communicator's authority and attractiveness) but also in the message itself. This section will describe three peripheral cues in your message that can appeal to people who are using heuristic processing.

*Amount of Information.* Consistent with the lazy nature of heuristic processing, we can easily be influenced by the sheer amount of supporting information that a message contains. Generally, people using heuristic processing will be more persuaded if you include more information in your message because they blindly assume that your message contains more support (Petty & Cacioppo, 1984).

Suppose that you're shopping online for a blender. Because this decision is relatively unimportant, your motivation to evaluate the descriptions of each blender would be fairly low, and you would likely use heuristic processing. If you stumble across a blender with a lengthy description and long list of benefits, you're more likely to assume that the extensive information implies a high-quality blender. If other blenders only offer a short description and list of benefits, you're likely to rely on the length of descriptions to assume that the blender with more information is a higher-quality blender.

If you know that your target will use heuristic processing to decide between a set of options, you can guide his choice by providing more information under the option that you want him to select. Even if that information doesn't necessarily support the benefit of that option, it can still influence your target's decision.

*Aesthetics.* Whether it occurs consciously or nonconsciously, people evaluate information based on the aesthetics of a message. Even important financial decisions, such as a financial analyst evaluating a company's annual reports, can be influenced by the design and graphics within those financial reports (Townsend & Shu, 2010).

A promising new field—called *neuroaesthetics*—studies brain responses toward aesthetically pleasing stimuli (Chatterjee, 2010). One of the main findings from this field is that people experience a biological sense of pleasure when they view aesthetically pleasing material. For example, when researchers measured people's neural responses when they viewed an assortment of paintings, they found that the orbitofrontal cortex (an area of our brain associated with rewards) became activated only for paintings that those people previously rated to be beautiful (Kawabata & Zeki, 2004).

Whenever we view aesthetically pleasing stimuli, our brain experiences a rewarding sensation, and we often misattribute that pleasurable feeling to the underlying content of that message. Therefore, you should always spend time enhancing the aesthetics of a message, even if it seems irrelevant.

Some marketers argue that website aesthetics are unimportant because "the only thing that matters is the strength of the content." Don't listen to those so-called marketing "gurus." Website aesthetics are crucial for a number of reasons. First, people use aesthetics as a heuristic for quality; if your website is aesthetically pleasing, they'll assume your content is above average, and vice versa. This benefit leads to a second benefit: aesthetics will influence website visitors to actually evaluate your content, a decision that's usually made within 50 milliseconds (Lindgaard et al., 2006). The strongest content in the world won't matter if people don't actually stop to evaluate it.

*Justification.* Would you mind reading this section while underlining it with your finger? Because that will help demonstrate the psychological principle in this section (I'll explain why in a few paragraphs).

Imagine that you're at a library. You're in a rush to use the copier, but you're waiting for someone to finish using it. Which of the following three requests do you think would help you the most?

➤ Excuse me, I have 5 pages. May I use the copier?
➤ Excuse me, I have 5 pages. May I use the copier, because I need to make some copies?
➤ Excuse me, I have 5 pages. May I use the copier, because I am in a rush?

Did you guess the third reason? Technically, you'd be right. In the classic study that examined this scenario, 94 percent complied with the third request, whereas only 60 percent complied with the first request (Langer, Blank, & Chanowitz, 1978).

But what about the second request? When you think about it, that request is virtually the same as the first request. If you need to use a copier, then *obviously* you need to make some copies; adding "because I have to make some copies" shouldn't make a difference.

What's fascinating, though, is that the second request yielded 93 percent compliance, a nearly identical rate of compliance as the third request. When people provide a reason for their request, people who are using heuristic processing will generally assume that the reason is valid. Therefore, giving *any* reason—even a meaningless reason such as "because I have to make some copies"—can enhance your persuasion because it becomes a heuristic that your target uses to decide whether he will comply.

Are you still reading while underlining the words with your finger? It would be impossible to force every single reader to comply with that request, but the justification that I used—"because that will help demonstrate the psychological principle in this section"—would have elicited a larger percentage of compliance because it was a form of justification, even though the reason was almost meaningless (why else would I ask you to do that task otherwise?).

Whenever you present a message or make a request, you should almost always provide some sort of justification, even if it seems trivial. If people are using heuristic processing, they will mindlessly assume that your reason is valid, and they will be more likely to accept your message or comply with your request.

I realize that there was a lot of information in this step of METHODS, so I made a diagram to summarize this step. You can refer to Figure 11.1 on the following page.

**Figure 11.1  Summary of Step 5**

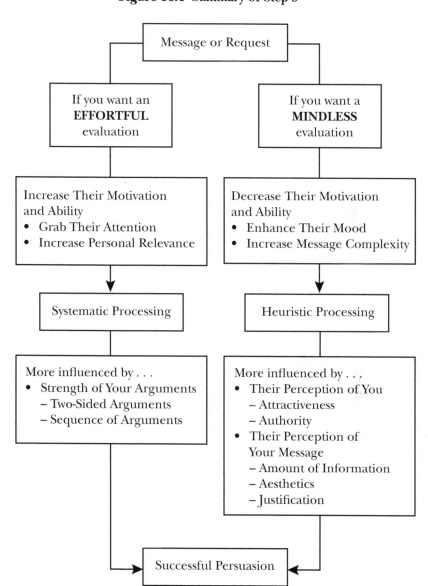

# REAL WORLD APPLICATION:
# HOW TO IMPRESS YOUR BOSS

As you prepare to leave work one day, your boss approaches your desk with a request: she asks you to prepare and deliver a PowerPoint presentation at 11:00 a.m. the following day. Although you're dead tired, you prepare a few slides and then leave. You plan to finish the rest of the slides the following morning before you present it.

That night, you set your alarm clock for 5:00 a.m. so that you can wake up early to finish the presentation. However, to your dismay, your alarm clock fails to work, and you wake up the following morning at 10:00 a.m. You rush to get ready, but you arrive to work late at 10:30 a.m.

You would need at least two hours to prepare a quality presentation, but you only have a half hour available. In order to determine the best focus of your time for that half hour, you casually stop by your boss's office to gauge her mood. To your surprise, she's in a rather pleasant mood, and she asks you how the presentation is coming along. Despite the panicking thoughts inside your head, you give her a resounding, "It's coming along great!"

Armed with the knowledge of her mood, you rush back to your desk and begin working hastily on the presentation. Because your boss's mood is pleasant, and because you studied the concepts in this book, you realize that your boss will be less critical of the actual underlying arguments in the presentation (i.e., she'll be relying heavily on heuristic processing). She'll also be influenced by other factors that are irrelevant to the actual arguments, such as the aesthetics of the presentation. Therefore, rather than try to create stronger support for the information that you put in the presentation the evening before, you decide to focus on enhancing the aesthetics of the presentation. You spend the next 20 minutes enhancing the color scheme, layout, and overall appearance of the PowerPoint slides. You're hoping that your boss's pleasant mood will lead her to view your aesthetically pleasing presentation and assume that the underlying content is equally as strong.

The time is now 10:50 a.m., and you have 10 minutes remaining before you must guide your boss through the presentation. At this point, you spend those remaining 10 minutes brainstorming clever and articulate ways to phrase the information that you've already compiled. Due to her reliance on heuristic processing, you should be able to convince your boss that the underlying arguments are strong if you can deliver them in an expressive and confident manner.

Ten minutes pass, and you go to your boss's office to guide her through the presentation. To your delight, your boss congratulates you on a stunning job, with additional compliments on the layout of the presentation. You end by letting your boss know that you'd be happy to investigate the topic further so that you can deliver a presentation with even stronger supporting evidence. She agrees, and you walk out of her office with a sigh of relief.

# STEP 6

# Drive Their Momentum

| | | | |
|---|---|---|---|
| **Before the Request** | *Step 1:* | **M** | Mold Their Perception |
| | *Step 2:* | **E** | Elicit Congruent Attitudes |
| | *Step 3:* | **T** | Trigger Social Pressure |
| | *Step 4:* | **H** | Habituate Your Message |
| **During the Request** | *Step 5:* | **O** | Optimize Your Message |
| | ***Step 6:*** | **D** | **Drive Their Momentum** |
| **After the Request** | *Step 7:* | **S** | Sustain Their Compliance |

## OVERVIEW:
## DRIVE THEIR MOMENTUM

Although you've now presented your request, you're not done yet. Rather than throw your request on the table and pray that your target complies, why not use a few psychological tactics to spark some more motivation?

The chapters within this step will explain two powerful techniques to further drive your target's momentum toward compliance. First, you'll learn how to give your target proper incentives (it's not as straightforward as it might seem). Second, you'll learn how to harness the power of limitations and "psychological reactance" to exert even more pressure. After implementing these tactics, you should receive their compliance (but if not, the final step in METHODS will help you out).

# CHAPTER 12

# Provide Proper Incentives

I rarely watch TV, but one night I was flipping through the channels when I stumbled upon an episode of the *Big Bang Theory*, an episode where Sheldon, the eccentric brainiac main character, was trying to influence the behavior of Penny, the female main character. Much like dog trainers reward their dogs with a treat after they perform a desired behavior, Sheldon offered Penny a chocolate each time that she performed a good deed (e.g., cleaned up his dirty dishes).

Although Sheldon's "positive reinforcement" successfully changed Penny's behavior throughout the course of the episode, could small rewards shape our behavior in real life? Though an amusing portrayal, that underlying psychological principle—*operant conditioning*—is actually very powerful. When used properly, rewards and incentives can nonconsciously guide people's behavior toward your intended goal.

But what's considered a "proper" incentive? As you'll learn in this chapter, many people make a few surprising errors when they use incentives to reward and motivate people. This chapter will teach you how to avoid those common mistakes so that you can offer incentives that will be successful at driving your target's momentum.

## THE POWER OF REWARDS

It all started in the 1930s with B. F. Skinner, the most well-known behavioral psychologist. He created what came to be known as a "Skinner box," a box that automatically rewarded a rat or pigeon each time they performed a desired behavior. After observing how those rewards caused his animals to express the corresponding behavior more often, he proposed his theory of operant conditioning to explain that behavior is guided by consequences; we tend to perform behavior that gets reinforced, and we tend to avoid behavior that gets punished (Skinner, 1938).

How powerful is reinforcement? One night, Skinner set the reward mechanism in several Skinner boxes to give pigeons a reward at predetermined time intervals. Even though the rewards were only based on time (i.e., not the pigeons' behavior), the pigeons nevertheless attributed those rewards to whichever behavior they were exuding immediately before those rewards. As Skinner described, their misattribution led to some peculiar behavior:

> One bird was conditioned to turn counter-clockwise about the cage, making two or three turns between reinforcements. Another repeatedly thrust its head into one of the upper corners of the cage. A third developed a "tossing" response, as if placing its head beneath an invisible bar and lifting it repeatedly. Two birds developed a pendulum motion of the head and body, in which the head was extended forward and swung from right to left with a sharp movement followed by a somewhat slower return. (Skinner, 1948)

You might find those behaviors somewhat amusing, but we're not that different from pigeons. Many of us actually perform similar behavior without realizing it.

Do you ever wonder why superstitions are so powerful? Why do so many of us perform a lucky ritual each time that we perform a certain action? For example, you might dribble a basketball three times—no more, no less—every time you shoot a foul shot because you think it brings you good luck. Are you insane? Nope. You were simply guided by the same forces that guide pigeons.

You can start to see the connection when you consider how that basketball ritual might have emerged in the first place. Suppose that you just made a foul shot after bouncing the ball three times. You jokingly attribute your success to bouncing the ball three times, and in your half-joking manner, you decide to bounce the ball three times for your next shot. And . . . *Swish.* Whaddya know, you make your shot again.

From this point forward, you start to gain more belief in that ritual, and so you perform it more often. Now that you're starting to develop the expectation that your ritual helps you make foul shots, you're more likely to trigger a placebo effect and actually make your shots more often when you perform that ritual. More importantly, your belief in that ritual will now perpetuate because it will continuously be reinforced through your increasingly successful foul shots. Much like a pigeon will perform odd behavior because it misattributes a reward to that specific behavior, you'll start to perform your arbitrary ritual more often because you will misattribute your successful shots to that ritual. See, we're not so different from pigeons.

## PERSUASION STRATEGY: PROVIDE PROPER INCENTIVES

This chapter breaks tradition by skipping the "why rewards are so powerful" section (the reason is explained in the final chapter). The rest of this chapter will focus on the practical applications of using incentives to reward and motivate your target.

First, offering any type of incentive will boost your persuasion, right? Wrong. Mounting research has disconfirmed the common dogma that all incentives lead to better performance. The main reason for that surprising discrepancy can be found in two types of motivation that result from different incentives:

➢ *Intrinsic motivation*—Motivation that emerges from a genuine personal desire (i.e., people perform a task because they find it interesting or enjoyable)
➢ *Extrinsic motivation*—Motivation that emerges for external reasons (i.e., people perform a task to receive a corresponding reward)

Because intrinsic motivation is generally more effective, this section will explain the types of incentives that extract intrinsic motivation from your target.

**Size of Incentive.** Common sense dictates that large incentives are more effective than small incentives. Intuitively, it makes sense; but that's not necessarily the case. Extensive research shows that small incentives can be more effective than large incentives in certain situations.

Perhaps the most direct reason why large incentives can be ineffective is that they sometimes increase anxiety levels. When people in one study were given incentives to perform tasks that measured creativity, memory, and motor skills, their performance sharply decreased when the incentive was very large because it caused them to "choke under pressure" (Ariely et al., 2009).

Does that mean that all large incentives are bad? Not at all. When incentives aren't so large as to increase anxiety levels, they *can* elicit higher levels of motivation and compliance. Uri Gneezy and Aldo Rustichini (2000a) conducted an experiment that attracted considerable attention from academia because of their surprising finding. They gathered a group of high school students to travel from house to house collecting donations, and they offered the students one of three different incentives:

> ➤ Large incentive (10 percent of the total money that they collected)
> ➤ Small incentive (1 percent of the total money that they collected)
> ➤ No incentive (just the same good ol' heartfelt speech about the importance of the donations)

Among those three incentives, which do you think elicited the most motivation from the students (in terms of the amount of money collected)?

Believe it or not, the students who received no incentive collected the most money (an average of NIS 239 collected). Students who received the large incentive were a close second (an average of NIS 219 collected), followed by the students who received the small incentive (a pathetic average of NIS 154). This surprising finding led the researchers to conclude that you should either "pay enough or don't pay at all."

But wait. Why did people in that study collect the most money when no incentive was given? The answer can be found in how people develop congruent attitudes from their behavior (Harmon-Jones, 2000). When people are guided by large external rewards, they develop the congruent attitude that they are merely performing that action because of the reward. However, when an incentive is small or nonexistent, people develop the congruent attitude that they are performing that action because of a personal desire (i.e., they develop intrinsic motivation).

Recall the study described in Chapter 5 where students developed a favorable attitude toward a boring experiment when they were paid $1 to lie to new participants and claim that it was fun (Festinger & Carlsmith, 1959). When students received only $1, this "insufficient justification" exerted more pressure on them to resolve their inconsistent behavior, and they resolved that dissonance by developing a genuinely positive attitude toward the experiment. In social psychology, this *less-leads-to-more effect* explains that smaller rewards can often be more effective because people develop a congruent attitude of intrinsic motivation to resolve their inconsistent behavior (Leippe & Eisenstadt, 1994).

This principle even influenced my own motivation to write this book. I started writing *Methods of Persuasion* while working at my past consulting job, and after writing it part-time for a few months, I took a large risk by quitting my job to focus on writing it full-time. Being fresh out of college, I had minimal savings, and so I worked endlessly for months to write this book, not because I *wanted* to but because I *needed* to launch it so that I could generate money to live, essentially. As soon as my intrinsic motivation became extrinsic, the task of writing this book—a task that I once found truly enjoyable—became something that I found very daunting and unpleasant.

My attitude became unfavorable because of the change in my motivation. While I was working on the book part-time, I was still putting in long hours, but I justified my hard work by developing the congruent attitude that I genuinely enjoyed writing it. But as soon I quit my job to write this book, I *needed* to write it so that I could generate income. And along with that very large external reward (essentially, money to survive) came the new congruent attitude that I was only writing the book for those external reasons. I'm very excited to finally launch this book and resume other income-generating activities so that my positive feeling toward writing can return.

So what's the takeaway? How big should your incentive be? When you want to persuade people to comply with a one-time act, then a large incentive might be your best bet (but not too large of an incentive that will cause them to "choke"). However, when you're trying to persuade people to develop a long-term change in their attitude or behavior, a large incentive will backfire because it will spark extrinsic motivation. They might comply with your request, but they will be less likely to develop a *genuinely* favorable attitude toward the task. In order to create the greatest change in your target's attitude, you need "insufficient justification"—your incentive must be small or nonexistent so that your target attributes his compliance toward a genuine desire to comply, not toward a desire to receive the external reward.

**Form of Incentive.** The second factor that you should consider is the form of incentive (e.g., monetary incentive) because, as you'll see, certain incentives will lead to certain types of motivation. This section will describe the two most common forms of incentives: monetary and social incentives.

*Monetary Incentives.* Albeit effective at driving extrinsic motivation, monetary incentives are very poor at eliciting intrinsic motivation.

Part of the reason for this failure stems from the negative connotation that we place on monetary incentives:

> Depending on their nature, incentives can shift a situation from a social to a monetary frame . . . You meet an attractive person, and in due time you tell that person, "I like you very much and would like to have sex with you." Alternatively, consider the same situation, but now you say, "I like you very much and would like to have sex with you, *and,* to sweeten the deal, I'm also willing to pay you $20!" Only a certain kind of economist would expect your partner to be happier in the second scenario. (Gneezy, Meier, & Rey-Biel, 2011, p. 11)

Without a doubt, monetary incentives (and especially cash incentives) can carry an incredibly negative connotation.

That notion is extremely important because, as Dan Ariely (2009) explains in *Predictably Irrational*, you need to be careful about turning a social relationship into a market relationship. Suppose that two friends offer to help you move into your new apartment. To thank them for their efforts, you give each of them a reward: for one friend, you buy her a bottle of wine (a social incentive), and for the other friend, you pay her $50 in cash (a monetary incentive).

Now fast-forward two weeks. A pipe bursts in your new home, and you need help cleaning your flooded basement. Which friend would be more likely to help? You guessed it. The friend that received the bottle of wine will feel a greater urge to maintain the social relationship, whereas the friend who received the cash will be more likely to expect another cash reward because you transformed that social relationship into a market relationship.

In order to maintain healthy social relationships, you should refrain from giving your friends cash, and instead, offer them a gift if you want to thank or reward them. As Dan Ariely describes, "while gifts are financially inefficient, they are an important social lubricant [because] they help us make friends and create long-term relationships . . . Sometimes, it turns out, a waste of money can be worth a lot" (Ariely, 2009).

The same outcome can occur when you use a monetary fine to discourage behavior. When researchers implemented a small fine for parents who were late to pick up their child from daycare, the amount of tardiness actually increased (Gneezy & Rustichini, 2000b). When they removed the fine, tardiness returned to zero. Why? That small fine transformed the social duty for parents to pick up their children on time into a market price. It essentially removed the guilt that parents would feel if they picked up their child late because it became a price that parents could pay for being tardy.

*Social Incentives.* In terms of intrinsic motivation, social rewards (e.g., gifts, praise, positive feedback) can be more powerful than monetary incentives because they avoid the negative connotation associated with money. Although offering $20 for sex would be highly frowned upon, "offering $20 worth of flowers might indeed make the desired partner happier" (Gneezy, Meier, & Rey-Biel, 2011).

Social incentives are powerful because they're more subtle than monetary incentives. Remember in the *Big Bang Theory* where Sheldon conditioned Penny's behavior by offering her a chocolate each time that she performed a desirable behavior? If the reward had been money, Sheldon's devious motive would have become crystal clear; chocolates helped to disguise his underlying motive.

Even more undetectable than chocolates, however, are social incentives that incorporate verbal praise or positive feedback. Putting that notion to the test, a pair of researchers from Harvard conducted a neat study where they called students to discuss their opinions about Harvard's educational system. Each time that a student mentioned a positive comment, the researcher on the phone responded with an affirmative "Good." Compared to a control group, students who received that verbal reinforcement developed a significantly more positive attitude toward the educational system by the end of the phone call (Hildum & Brown, 1956). Even rewards as small as verbal acknowledgement can help you nonconsciously guide someone's attitude toward your desired goal.

**Perception of Incentives.** The size and form of your incentive are important factors, but there's a third and more important factor: your target's perception of your incentive.

Sometimes, the mere presence of an incentive can communicate negative information. For example, offering people an incentive could lead them to perceive that you distrust their competence in completing a task or that you're trying to control their behavior. In these situations, those incentives can lead to worse performance (Falk & Kosfeld, 2006).

In fact, those two examples—a perceived lack of competence and a perceived lack of autonomy—are the two most commonly cited perceptions that determine whether your incentive will elicit intrinsic or extrinsic motivation (Deci & Ryan, 1980). This section will explain those two perceptions in more detail and how you can overcome them.

*Competence.* How can you offer incentives that won't make it seem like you distrust your target's competence? Perhaps the best solution lies in the "contingency" of your incentive. Generally, there are two main types of incentives:

➤ *Engagement-contingent:* an incentive that is given for engaging in an activity (e.g., parents rewarding their child if she studies for an exam)
➤ *Performance-contingent:* an incentive that is given only if some standard of performance is met (e.g., parents rewarding their child if she earns a high score on an exam)

According to researchers, engagement-contingent rewards result in worse performance because they devalue your target's competence, whereas performance-contingent rewards result in higher performance because they promote competence (Houlfort et al., 2002).

*Autonomy.* If your target perceives your incentive as an attempt to control her behavior, then she's more likely to develop extrinsic motivation (if any motivation at all). Even simple phrasing, such as the word "should" (e.g., "you should do _____ for _____"), can trigger feelings of control and worsen performance (Ryan, 1982).

In addition to avoiding the word "should," how else can you provide an incentive without infringing on your target's autonomy? One powerful and clever idea is to let your target choose an incentive from a list of potential options. For example, whereas most businesses simply provide their salespeople with a predetermined monetary commission rate, it might be more favorable to let their salespeople choose the type of commission that they want (e.g., monetary commission, vacations days, gift certificates).

Allowing people to choose their commission or incentive, in any situation, can lead to three powerful benefits:

> First, rather than trying to guess which incentive will spark the greatest motivation in your target, allowing your target to choose among multiple incentives will lead to an incentive that is more appealing to your target (e.g., some salespeople might prefer a monetary commission, whereas others might prefer vacation days).

> Second, allowing your targets to choose will satisfy their need for autonomy, an outcome that will spark more intrinsic motivation and, as a result, higher job satisfaction and performance levels.

> Third, their choice becomes a type of behavior that reinforces a congruent attitude that they genuinely want the incentive. Not working hard enough to achieve that incentive would be inconsistent with their new attitude, and so they will be motivated to work

harder so that they can achieve it (e.g., when salespeople choose vacation days as their commission, they reinforce the idea that vacation days are important to them, and they will be motivated to work harder to achieve that incentive).

Don't brush over this advice. This particular strategy involving choice is greatly overlooked by both academia and industry professionals, which is mind-boggling given the persuasive psychological mechanisms at play.

I applied this concept to commissions for salespeople, but the applications are endless. Recent research has shown that choice can also motivate students to do their homework, a task that rarely elicits intrinsic motivation. For centuries, homework has failed to extract intrinsic motivation because it doesn't promote autonomy; students feel like they're *required* to do it (which is true). Some radical proponents have suggested that homework should be optional, but there's a more effective strategy: teachers should give students a list of potential assignments, and they should allow them to choose which one they want to complete.

It's amazing how much of a difference teachers can make when they offer their students a choice of homework assignments. In a recent study, Patall, Copoer, and Wynn (2010) found that this choice for high school students led to:

➤ Higher interest and enjoyment in doing homework
➤ Higher confidence and competence in the material
➤ Higher completion rates of assignments
➤ Higher scores on corresponding exams

To spur the most momentum from your target, you need to maintain people's intrinsic motivation by promoting their competence and perceived sense of freedom, a task that can be accomplished through framing your incentive and allowing your target to choose a particular incentive or request.

As you'll learn in the next chapter, a perceived sense of freedom is a powerful principle that has other persuasion applications. The next chapter explains a few other strategies you can use to take advantage of that principle to trigger even more momentum from your target.

# CHAPTER 13

# Motivate
# Through Limitations

Do *not* read this chapter. Skip directly to the next chapter, and don't *ever* come back to read this chapter.

What are you doing? Why are you still reading when I deliberately told you to skip to the next chapter? What's the psychological force behind your motivation? There are two main forces that are guiding your behavior right now:

1. Your curiosity became aroused when I tried to stop you from reading further.
2. I limited your autonomy and freedom, which caused you to actively fight that limitation.

This chapter will teach you how to use the second reason to boost your persuasion. Specifically, you'll learn why limiting someone's freedom can become a powerful motivator, and you'll learn clever strategies to use that concept to further drive your target's momentum.

## THE POWER OF LIMITATIONS

You're eating dinner with your family when it suddenly appears. Right in front of you appears the most marvelous entity that your mere human eyes have ever witnessed. It's magnificent. It's majestic. It's, dare I say, beautiful. It's the very last slice of pizza.

Part of you wonders how that slice became so valuable within such a short period of time. But that part of you quickly gets shoved aside by the part of you that simply *needs to have it*. There's no time to question your motive; you have more important things to worry about, like the other vultures sitting around the table.

But you can't appear *too* hasty. You need to plan your strike carefully. As you casually quicken your eating pace to finish your current slice, you discreetly shift your gaze toward your sister, the person that you perceive to pose the greatest threat. Through your peripheral vision— a type of vision that you *need* to use in such dire circumstances—you see her eyeing the last slice. Uh-oh. Time to move fast.

You start to scarf down the remainder of your slice, but it's becoming too late. In what seems to be slow motion, your sister reaches her hand toward the middle of the table, picks up that last slice, and brings it back to her own plate. Ugh. You failed.

Oh well. You resolve your dissonance by reminding yourself that you already ate 4 slices and that you're completely stuffed anyway.

## WHY ARE LIMITATIONS SO POWERFUL?

So, why *did* that slice of pizza become valuable when it was the last slice? Or for that matter, why does *any* piece of food—whether it's a box of chocolates or a bin of cookies—become more valuable when there's only one piece left? This section will explain three principles behind that phenomenon: psychological reactance, loss aversion, and commodity theory.

**Psychological Reactance.** To understand the answer behind the pizza phenomenon, it'll help if you recognize how it's similar to the first illustration in this chapter where I asked you to immediately skip to the next chapter.

In both illustrations, one of your freedoms was limited. In the opening example, I limited your freedom to read this chapter; in the second example, I limited your freedom to eat pizza. Do you see the common outcome? Whenever a freedom becomes limited, we react. Literally. It's called *psychological reactance* (Brehm, 1966). When we perceive a particular freedom becoming restricted, we feel a natural tendency to maintain or recapture that freedom.

Have you ever wondered why some teenagers, after being told by their parents that they can't date a specific person, want to date that person even more? When teenagers perceive their parents to be controlling their behavior, they're more likely to engage in psychological reactance by touting the infamous, "You can't control me! I can make my own decisions!" Indeed, reactance can explain why teenagers constantly battle their controlling parents and why warning labels on violent television programs actually increase viewership (Bushman & Stack, 1996).

Like most principles in this book, psychological reactance is so strong that it can exert its influence on a nonconscious level. To demonstrate, place yourself in the shoes of participants in a clever experiment (Chartrand, Dalton, & Fitzsimons, 2007). Think of people in your life that you perceive to be very controlling. Now, among that list of controlling people, choose one person who typically wants you to work hard and one person who typically wants you to have fun.

Researchers in that experiment subtly extracted that information from students so that they could examine how they would perform on an intellectual task after being subliminally exposed to those names. Remarkably, even though participants weren't able to consciously notice the names of those controlling people, they still engaged in psychological reactance. People performed significantly worse on the intellectual task when they were primed with the name that they associated with working hard, whereas people performed significantly better when they were primed with the name that they associated with having fun. Psychological reactance is so strong that it occurs automatically and outside of our conscious awareness.

**Loss Aversion.** I hate to spring this upon you, but you need to make a life-or-death decision right now. There's a spreading disease that can potentially kill 600 people, and you need to choose between two pre-vention programs:

➤ **Program A:** A total of 200 people will be saved.
➤ **Program B:** There is a 33% chance that all 600 people will be saved, but there is a 67% chance that nobody will be saved.

When presented with those two hypothetical options, most people chose Program A because the idea of saving 200 people seemed very promising (whereas gambling with people's lives seemed too risky).

But let's change the programs a bit. Forget Program A and B. Pre-tend you never even read them. Instead, imagine that you needed to choose between the following two options:

➤ **Program C:** A total of 400 people will die.
➤ **Program D:** There is a 33% chance that nobody will die, but there is a 67% chance that 600 people will die.

Which option would you choose? Like most people, you probably felt compelled to choose Program D, which is exactly what most people chose in the original experiment (Tversky & Kahneman, 1981).

But there's something interesting about those programs. Did you notice that the second set of programs was exactly the same as the first? Program A is identical to Program C, and Program B is identical to Program D; the only difference was the wording of the programs and the emphasis on saving versus losing lives.

Since those two sets of programs were exactly the same, why did the results flip when people were presented with the second set of options? The answer: the pressure to avoid a loss overpowers the pres-sure to achieve a gain (Tversky & Kahneman, 1991).

We all feel an instinctive urge to avoid losses, including the loss of an opportunity. When there's only one slice of pizza remaining, we feel an increased pressure to seize that last slice before we lose the opportunity. Instead of viewing the slice of pizza through a lens of freedom (such as through psychological reactance), loss aversion views that pizza scenario in terms of a possible lost opportunity, a similar idea but a distinction nonetheless.

**Commodity Theory.** In the pizza anecdote, there was a third factor that compelled you to want that last slice: commodity theory (Brock, 1968). This theory proposes that people place higher value on something when it's perceived to be limited and unavailable, compared to when it's plentiful and abundant.

A group of researchers applied the same pizza concept to chocolate chip cookies. When people were presented with a jar containing two cookies, they rated the taste of the cookies higher than a group of people who were given a jar containing ten of those cookies (Worchel, Lee, & Adewole, 1975). Not only were you more compelled to take the last slice of pizza, but this principle suggests that you might have also enjoyed it more.

Commodity theory is so robust that it applies to other contexts besides food. In addition to the commonly cited "drunk goggles" reason, commodity theory can explain why men in bars tend to find women more attractive as the night progresses (Madey et al., 1996). At the beginning of the night, the opportunity to score a date is promising, but as the night wears on, that opportunity gradually shrinks. As the end of the night gets even closer, that opportunity becomes even more limited, which causes men to find the remaining women more attractive.

## PERSUASION STRATEGY: MOTIVATE THROUGH LIMITATIONS

To summarize the chapter so far, there are three ways in which limitations influence perception and behavior:

1.  When we perceive a freedom becoming limited, we feel an urge to engage in psychological reactance to reclaim that freedom (e.g.,

when our freedom to eat pizza becomes limited, we feel a stronger desire to reclaim that freedom by eating pizza).

2.  We are psychologically wired to avoid loss; when an opportunity is becoming limited, we feel a pressure to seize that opportunity to avoid losing it (e.g., when our opportunity to eat pizza is diminishing, we feel compelled to seize that last slice).

3.  When we perceive something to be limited, scarce, or unavailable, we place higher value on the item in question (e.g., a slice of pizza becomes more valuable when it is the only slice left).

Albeit similar, psychological reactance, loss aversion, and commodity theory can explain why limitations are so powerful. Now that you understand these principles, the next section will explain how you can use them to drive more momentum from your target.

**Limit Their Options.** The previous chapter described how allowing your target to choose an incentive can help spark intrinsic motivation because it promotes their freedom. Although the previous chapter described choice as a good thing, choice can become a detriment when there are *too many* options from which to choose. Popularized by Barry Schwartz (2004), this *paradox of choice* can lead to two negative outcomes: (1) people are less satisfied with their decision, or (2) people avoid deciding altogether.

Take a look at the following two sets of options:

**Set 1**
Option A
Option B
Option C

**Set 2**
Option A
Option B
Option C

Option D
Option E
Option F
Option G
Option H
Option I
Option J

Those options could represent anything (e.g., different brands of jeans that a clothing store sells, number of houses that a real estate broker shows a client). For the sake of the example, imagine that each set represents different mutual funds that an investment firm offers its customers. As you can see, one firm offers a limited number of options (Set 1), whereas another firm offers a plethora of options (Set 2). The remainder of this section will use this hypothetical example to explain the two negative outcomes that can occur with too many options.

*Outcome 1: Lower Satisfaction with Decision.* There are two main reasons why offering too many options can cause people to feel less satisfied with their final decision.

First, when you increase the number of options, you also increase people's expectations for the quality of the final option. When the number of options surpasses a certain point, people's heightened expectations may become an extreme anchor point that triggers a contrast effect and causes the final option to seem below average (Diehl & Lamberton, 2008).

The second reason stems from loss aversion. Take a look at the following two gambling situations:

1. There is a 90% chance you will win $10, but there is a 10% chance you will win nothing.
2. There is a 90% chance you will win $1 million, but there is a 10% chance you will win nothing.

In both situations, the loss is the same: you win nothing. Since each loss is exactly the same, any rational human being should feel exactly the same with each loss. But it's crystal clear that those losses would result in very different feelings; you'd probably forget the $10 loss immediately, but the $1 million loss will drive you crazy.

How does that relate to presenting options? You should first recognize that, typically, any option naturally offers unique benefits and drawbacks compared to other options. In our mutual fund example, some mutual funds would offer certain benefits that aren't offered in other funds, and vice versa. Due to these natural tradeoffs, any option that you choose must naturally forgo certain benefits that are offered only in other funds. Your dissatisfaction enters the equation once you recognize that, when you make your decision, you're *losing* some benefits that are only offered in other funds.

Recall how the loss of $1 million drove you crazy, whereas the loss of $10 was forgotten immediately. That underlying concept applies here. Your loss seems more severe when more options are present because you seem to lose more potential benefits. If you choose Option A in the first set of mutual fund options, you only lose the benefits from Option B and C, but if you choose Option A in the second set, you lose the benefits that are offered in all of the 9 remaining options. Though you chose the same option in each set, the loss of additional benefits seems more severe in the second set, which causes you to be less satisfied with your decision.

Essentially, this situation triggers cognitive dissonance. On one hand, you see attractive benefits that are being offered in other options, but on the other hand, you actively give up those benefits by choosing only one option. That inconsistency leads to a feeling of discomfort and dissatisfaction with your decision.

In the consumer domain, we resolve that *postpurchase dissonance*—a more specific form of cognitive dissonance that applies to consumer purchases—in a number of different ways. For example, after our purchase, we might place greater importance on our product's distinctive features (Gawronski, Bodenhausen, & Becker, 2007). However, we *do* typically resolve that discomfort, so the dissatisfaction that results from presenting too many options isn't a *huge* problem. The bigger problem stems from the second negative outcome of the paradox of choice: decision paralysis.

*Outcome 2: Decision Paralysis.* There are two main reasons why presenting more options can cause people to avoid making a decision altogether.

The first reason is simply an extension of loss aversion: when facing a vast number of options, people recognize the potential loss that will result upon choosing only one option, and so they avoid that potential loss by postponing their decision.

The second reason is known as *information overload*. When you present more options to people, you place more cognitive strain on your target to investigate each option to make an informed decision, which can be very demotivating, especially when the decision is complex or important.

Did your employer ever present you with an extensive list of possible 401(k) plans? If so, you might have felt overwhelmed, and if you postponed your decision, you're not alone. Research shows that participation rates in 401(k) plans decrease in direct accordance with the number of plan options; the more options that are available, the lower the participation rate (Iyengar, Jiang, & Huberman, 2004).

*Solution.* I know it might sound like I'm discouraging you from presenting more options, but that's not the case. More choice is generally a good thing. As you learned in the previous chapter, presenting more options can lead to greater personal freedom, and it can also lead to a better solution to your issue (even though you might be less satisfied with your decision).

So why did I spend this entire section bashing choice when I'm now saying that more options are good? Despite this seemingly contradictory advice, the best strategy doesn't change the number of options;

it changes the number of *perceived* options. To demonstrate, try and remember this sequence of numbers:

7813143425

Remembering that sequence is doable, but difficult. But look at how much easier it becomes when you use a memory strategy known as "chunking" to divide those numbers into chunks:

781–314–3425

Yep, you guessed it. That's a standard U.S. phone number. It's amazing how much easier it becomes to remember a sequence of numbers when you separate those numbers into groups.

Although our working memory can only hold 5–9 pieces of information at a given time, the previous "chunks" are considered one piece of information, and so it becomes much easier for our brain to remember a sequence of numbers when it's divided into groups (Miller, 1956).

Applying that concept to persuasion, you can prevent the two negative outcomes of the paradox of choice by grouping your options into categories (Mogilner, Rudnick, & Iyengar, 2008). By categorizing your options into groups, not only do you minimize the perceived loss of the other options, but you also reduce information overload.

Remember Set 2 that contained a large number of mutual funds? You could divide those original 10 options into one of three risk categories:

**Set 2**
Low Risk
Option A
Option B
Option C

Medium Risk
Option D
Option E
Option F
Option G

High Risk
Option H
Option I
Option J

Much like how adding chunks in the phone number reduced information overload, organizing the funds into three risk categories reduces cognitive strain because they combine the options into groups. Instead of viewing 10 different options, people essentially perceive 3 options now, even though the number of options never really changed. Research has even confirmed that adding category labels, even if they're completely arbitrary, can make a list of options seem more appealing (a principle known as the *mere categorization effect*; Mogilner, Rudnick, & Iyengar, 2008).

Limiting the number of perceived options isn't the only way to prevent decision paralysis. The next strategy will explain other ways in which you can use limitations to spur more momentum from your target.

**Prevent Their Procrastination.** Albeit powerful, decision paralysis can be avoided. This section will teach you two limitations that you can implement to force your target to make a decision sooner rather than later.

*Limit Time.* The first technique is to limit the amount of time available to comply with your request, which can easily be accomplished by setting a deadline.

Question: Which day of the week is the least effective at gaining
   compliance?
Answer: Tomorrow.

There's something magical about tomorrow; it just never seems to
come. No matter how many days go by, tomorrow forever remains at the
same distance in the future. It's quite magical. Setting a deadline is so
powerful because it puts an end to that black magic by finally bringing
"tomorrow" closer to the present. Even if the deadline is irrelevant or
pulled from thin air, this time pressure can prevent procrastination.

Suppose that you're tired one night and you want to persuade
your spouse—a procrastinator by nature—to wash the dishes. You can
increase your chances remarkably by setting a specific deadline (e.g.,
by 8:00 p.m. that night). Though this deadline might be irrelevant, it
essentially starts the countdown timer and helps prevent your target
from procrastinating.

Deadlines are also very powerful because they limit a potential
opportunity; once the deadline passes, your target gives up that
opportunity. Sure, washing dishes may not be perceived as a once-
in-a-lifetime opportunity, but there *are* many other situations where
a deadline *can* make your message seem much more desirable (e.g.,
marketers setting deadlines for product coupons and discounts).

*Limit Availability.* You're walking down the aisle of a liquor store looking for some white wine, and you reach the shelves that are displaying the wine. There are two brands left—both of which are the same
price—but since you know nothing about wine, you're clueless about
which brand is better. What would you do in this scenario? Research
on shelf-based scarcity suggests that you would likely choose the brand
of wine with fewer bottles on the shelf (Parker & Lehmann, 2011).

If something is less available, people are more likely to spring to
action for two reasons: (1) they need to act fast before they lose the
opportunity (loss aversion), and (2) if the item is scarce, people assume

that it must be popular (commodity theory and an indirect influence of social pressure).

You might think that this concept only applies to selling products, but there are many other applications. This principle can even help you when you're applying for a job. Job applicants who indicate that they are considering other job opportunities (i.e., applicants who seem less available) are evaluated more favorably than candidates who don't indicate whether they're considering other job opportunities (Williams et al., 1993). Consistent with commodity theory, interviewers consciously or nonconsciously use availability as a heuristic to judge the quality of an applicant; if applicants are less available because they are considering other job offers, then they *must* be a better quality applicant.

## A MAGICIAN'S PERSPECTIVE: MISDIRECTING THE AUDIENCE'S ATTENTION

Having performed as a stage magician for many years, I can confidently say that one of the most fundamental principles of stage magic is *misdirection*: controlling the audience's attention to avoid seeing the "magic" occurring behind the scenes.

Despite that basic definition, performers interpret misdirection differently. Amateurs claim that misdirection is directing the audience's attention *away* from the secret (e.g., sleight of hand), whereas professionals claim that misdirection is directing the audience's attention *toward* something else.

Aren't those interpretations the same? That's what I thought for many years until I started recognizing the importance of limitations. Notice that amateurs try to *limit* the audience's attention toward the place where they shouldn't be looking, whereas professionals try to *direct* the audience's attention toward something else. As you learned in this chapter, whenever a freedom becomes limited, we feel a natural urge to resist that limitation. Thus, amateurs who try to limit the audience's attention are unintentionally creating more attention in that area.

Suppose that a magician is performing a trick where he makes a coin disappear. The entire trick rests on his ability to pretend that he places the coin in his left hand (but he actually retains the coin in his right hand). An amateur magician will be so focused on limiting the attention on his right hand that his actions will attract even more attention. For one, his peripheral vision will be focused on his right hand, an action that will cause the audience to direct their attention toward that spot. Even further, his hand will be more cramped because he'll be trying harder to shield the audience's view, a position that will look so unnatural that it will do nothing else but to attract *even more* attention toward his hand.

Compare that amateur to a professional who, instead, focuses on directing the audience's attention *toward* his left hand. When he focuses solely on his left hand—the hand that supposedly has the coin—his full focus will cause the audience to place their entire focus on his left hand. Rather than pull his right hand (which secretly holds the coin) away from his left hand, professionals will move their left hand away from their right hand. This movement and focus on the left hand captures the audience's attention, and their focus will inevitably be distracted from the magician's right hand. The result: the magician slowly opens his left hand to reveal that the coin has disappeared, triggering a miraculous feeling in the audience. Even in magic, understanding limitations can help create a miraculous moment.

# REAL WORLD APPLICATION:
# SELLING T-SHIRTS ONLINE

Suppose that you're selling T-shirts via an e-commerce website and that your company can design a huge selection of T-shirts, including different types, colors, and designs. Rather than post an image of each T-shirt combination on your website, you could guide website visitors through a three-step process that categorizes those T-shirt combinations.

In the first step, visitors could choose the T-shirt *type(s)* that they're interested in purchasing (e.g., short sleeve, long sleeve, etc.). Next, they could select the T-shirt *color(s)* that they're interested in purchasing. Third, they could choose the T-shirt *design(s)* that they're interested in purchasing (e.g., graphic tee, athletic, etc.)

After making those choices, they can be presented with a list of all T-shirt options that fit their criteria, and those options could be organized into groups of price ranges. That step-by-step process has many benefits:

➢ First, it substantially reduces the number of final options, which helps to reduce the perceived loss of other T-shirt options.

➢ Second, people choose among categories of options (e.g., type, color, design, and price range). Research has confirmed that the mere presence of categories increases customer satisfaction because it serves as a cue for greater variety (Mogilner, Rudnick, & Iyengar, 2008).

➢ Third, people are making a few choices among a manageable number of options (e.g., choosing short sleeve versus long sleeve) rather than making one choice among *all* possible T-shirt combinations. This setup helps reduce information overload because the options are more manageable within those categories.

➢ Fourth, because people are making numerous choices, you promote their autonomy and give them a personal feeling of control.

➤ Fifth, each consecutive choice is an action that helps them develop a congruent attitude that they're interested in purchasing a T-shirt. Once they develop that attitude, they will be motivated to act in a manner consistent with that attitude (i.e., by purchasing a T-shirt). If you were to simply present a list of options, people won't feel as committed to purchasing a T-shirt because they will not have performed an action or behavior to suggest that they're interested in purchasing one (except for merely visiting the website).

# STEP 7

# Sustain Their Compliance

| | | | |
|---|---|---|---|
| **Before the Request** | *Step 1:* | **M** | Mold Their Perception |
| | *Step 2:* | **E** | Elicit Congruent Attitudes |
| | *Step 3:* | **T** | Trigger Social Pressure |
| | *Step 4:* | **H** | Habituate Your Message |
| **During the Request** | *Step 5:* | **O** | Optimize Your Message |
| | *Step 6:* | **D** | Drive Their Momentum |
| **After the Request** | ***Step 7:*** | **S** | **Sustain Their Compliance** |

## OVERVIEW:
## SUSTAIN THEIR COMPLIANCE

So what was the verdict? Did your target comply with your request? Whether or not your target complied, you should still use the strategies in this seventh step of METHODS. The purpose of this step is two-fold. You can:

1.  Use these strategies to sustain your target's compliance, or . . .
2.  Use these strategies on an ongoing basis if you failed to secure their compliance.

Assuming that your target complied, there are many situations where you need to maintain that compliance, especially if your request involves a long-term change in behavior (e.g., trying to influence your spouse to eat healthier).

And if you still haven't gained their compliance, don't fret. You can use the strategies in this step to continuously exert pressure on your target over time so that they eventually cave and comply with your request. When your request has no strict deadline, there's no end to the persuasion process.

# CHAPTER 14

# Make Favorable Associations

As you could probably predict after learning about the recency effect in Chapter 11, I purposely ensured that this last chapter was very interesting and important (which is my attempt to leave you with a lasting positive memory for this book). Although it's presented last, this chapter actually forms the basis of the entire book because it encompasses schemas and priming, the topic of the very first chapter. Once you read this chapter, you'll understand why METHODS isn't a linear step-by-step sequence, but rather, a circular and ongoing process.

What's this chapter about? Some random food products can help explain. Mentally rate each of the three items in the following image in terms of how much you enjoy consuming it (1 = not at all, 10 = very much).

If you can't tell by looking at the image, the three products (from left to right) are oatmeal, mayonnaise, and coffee.

Do you have your rating? You may not have consciously realized it, but the mayonnaise in the middle likely affected your rating of the outer products (i.e., the oatmeal and the coffee). Why? Research shows that mayonnaise can spark feelings of "disgust," which can then be transferred to other products that are in contact with that item, an effect known as *product contagion.*

In a series of experiments examining product contagion, Morales and Fitzsimons (2007) presented people with a small shopping cart containing a few items, and they positioned some "feminine napkins" so that they were resting slightly on a box of cookies in that shopping cart. Even though everything was still packaged and unopened, the researchers discovered that this slight contact made people significantly less likely to want to try those cookies. When they presented a different group of people with those same items but with six inches of space between those products, that negative perception virtually disappeared. The researchers also found that product contagion occurs when the target item is non-consumable (e.g., notebooks) and that the effect becomes stronger when the packaging of the disgusting item is clear or transparent.

The main point I'm trying to illustrate with that study is that certain features from one stimulus can easily transfer to another stimulus, an implication that stems far beyond proper shelving in supermarkets. This chapter will explain a similar psychological principle and how you can transfer favorable qualities to your message via some type of association with another stimulus.

## WHY ARE ASSOCIATIONS SO POWERFUL?

It all started with a group of dogs. Dogs? Yep, dogs. Pavlov's dogs, to be more precise.

In 1927, Ivan Pavlov, the founder of what would become the most fundamental principle in all of psychology, stumbled upon his discovery when he was researching digestion in laboratory dogs (a very lucky accident for the field of psychology). He started noticing that whenever the lab assistant would enter the room with meat powder for the dogs, the dogs would start to salivate even before they could see or smell the meat. Like any rational researcher, Pavlov assumed that the dogs didn't possess some type of telepathic power but were instead being influenced by some scientific principle. And his hunch was right.

After developing the belief that the dogs were somehow being conditioned to *expect* the arrival of the meat, Pavlov conducted a series of experiments to test his prediction. He first examined whether his dogs would respond to a neutral stimulus, such as the ringing of a bell. When no particular response occurred, he started pairing the bell with the presentation of the meat powder; immediately before presenting the dogs with meat powder, he would repeatedly ring the bell. Before long, the dogs started associating the bell with the meat, and they would start to salivate upon Pavlov merely ringing the bell. Thus, he found:

Bell → No Salivation
Bell + Meat → Salivation
Bell → Salivation

Pavlov concluded that a neutral stimulus that elicits no behavioral response (e.g., a bell) can start to elicit a response if it becomes paired with an "unconditioned stimulus," a stimulus that *does* elicit a natural response (e.g., meat that elicits salivation). Albeit a simple finding, that idea of *classical conditioning* launched a new era in psychology.

Why does it work? The most common explanation is that if a neutral stimulus (e.g., bell) is repeatedly presented before an unconditioned stimulus (e.g., meat), then the neutral stimulus becomes a signal that the unconditioned stimulus is arriving (Baeyens et al., 1992). When Pavlov repeatedly rang the bell before presenting the meat, the dogs became conditioned to *expect* the arrival of the meat, and so they began salivating with a mere ring of the bell.

But that's not the only explanation. Far from it, in fact. Although the neutral stimulus is typically presented before the unconditioned stimulus, research shows that conditioning can occur even if the unconditioned stimulus (the response-provoking stimulus) is presented before the neutral stimulus, a form of classical conditioning known as *backward conditioning* or *affective priming* (Krosnick et al., 1992). If you present an unconditioned stimulus that elicits some type of affective/emotional state, you are essentially priming people to view a subsequent neutral stimulus through the lens of their new emotional mindset (hence the term "affective priming"). Accordingly, those emotional feelings can influence people's perception and evaluation of that neutral stimulus.

Suppose that you consistently phone your friend when the weather is beautiful. In this situation, you would be using affective priming to associate yourself with beautiful weather:

> You → No Response
> You + Beautiful Weather → Positive Response
> You → Positive Response

With enough pairings, your target would begin to associate the positive feelings that naturally occur from the beautiful weather with you. In other words, you become the bell from Pavlov's experiment, except instead of producing salivation, you'll produce a positive emotion when your target sees you.

Besides affective priming, there are other reasons why your target would come to associate you with the positive emotions produced from beautiful weather. The rest of this section will describe two additional explanations.

*Misattribution.* One of the main ideas that you should take away from this book is that we tend to make misattributions. Take processing fluency as an example. That principle can explain why stocks with easy-to-pronounce ticker symbols (e.g., KAR) significantly outperform stocks with ticker symbols that are difficult to pronounce (e.g., RDO)

(Alter & Oppenheimer, 2006). People mistakenly attribute the ease with which they process a ticker symbol with the strength of a company's financials; if a ticker symbol is easy to pronounce, the positive feelings that emerge from that quick processing get misattributed to the underlying financials of that company.

In classical conditioning, we make similar misattributions (Jones, Fazio, & Olson, 2010). If two stimuli become associated with each other, we can misattribute the feelings produced from one stimulus as stemming from the other stimulus. When we view humorous advertisements, for instance, we tend to misattribute the positive emotions that we experience from the humor as emerging from the product being advertised (Strick et al., 2011).

Remember the example where you (the neutral stimulus) associated yourself with good weather (the unconditioned stimulus)? Like some readers, you might have quickly brushed over that tidbit because it seemed far-fetched (let's face it, it does *seem* far-fetched). But research suggests that this claim may have some merit. Schwarz and Clore (1983) telephoned people on either a sunny or rainy day to assess their well-being, and remarkably, people were significantly happier and more satisfied with their life when the weather was sunny. But what's interesting is that the misattribution error disappeared for many people when the researchers began the conversation by asking, "How's the weather down there?" When people in the rainy condition were asked that innocent question, they consciously or nonconsciously realized that their dampened mood was due to the weather, and they adjusted their happiness ratings upward.

Here's the main takeaway: associations are powerful because we can easily misattribute characteristics and responses from one stimulus as emerging from another stimulus (and if you're thinking about calling up an old friend, it might not be a bad idea to wait until the weather is nice). The next section will explain one final reason behind the power of associations: our semantic network.

*Semantic Network.* As Chapter 1 explained, our brain has a semantic network, an interconnected web of knowledge containing everything that we've learned over time, and every concept (or "node") in that network is connected to other concepts that are similar or associated. Further, when one concept becomes activated, all other connected concepts become activated as well, a principle known as spreading activation. All of that was discussed in the first chapter.

This final chapter truly comes full-circle because associations can explain how that semantic network came into existence. Every concept that we've learned over time (i.e., every node in our semantic network) has emerged through an association. Whenever we're presented with a new concept, we can't simply place that concept free-floating in our brain; in order to successfully integrate that new concept into our existing network of knowledge, we need to attach it to an already existing concept via some type of similarity or association.

To illustrate, read the following passage that researchers gave to people in a clever research study:

> The procedure is actually quite simple. First you arrange things into different groups depending on their makeup. Of course, one pile may be sufficient depending on how much there is to do. If you have to go somewhere else due to lack of facilities that is the next step, otherwise you are pretty well set. It is important not to overdo any particular endeavor. That is, it is better to do too few things at once than too many. In the short run, this may not seem important, but complications from doing too many can easily arise. A mistake can be expensive as well. The manipulation of the appropriate mechanisms should be self-explanatory, and we need not dwell on it here. At first the whole procedure will seem complicated. Soon, however, it will become just another facet of life. It is difficult to foresee any end to the necessity for this task in the immediate future, but then one never can tell. (Bransford & Johnson, 1972, p. 722)

Like most people, you probably learned nothing from reading that excerpt. How could anyone make sense of such a confusing and oddly worded passage? However, if you knew the proper context of the information, you could then categorize that information under a relevant schema, and the passage would then become crystal clear. Here's the context of that passage: doing laundry. Now that you know the context, you could reread that passage and fully comprehend it because you can place that information under your schema of doing laundry.

Is this information starting to ring a bell? It should. In the first chapter, I explained that mentioning the concept of "luck" and "dwarf" can make the number seven more readily available on a nonconscious level. Due to the connections that exist between those two concepts and the number seven in our semantic network, the activation can spread from those concepts to the number seven.

A similar process occurs with classical conditioning. See Figure 14.1 for a snapshot of a more complex, yet still extremely simplified, version of our semantic network.

**Figure 14.1**

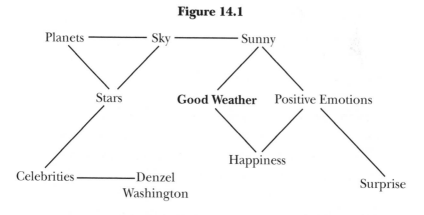

Classical conditioning is effective because it essentially forms a new connection in that network. When you consistently pair yourself with good weather, for example, you form a new connection between "Good Weather" and "You" in your target's semantic network (the more pairings, the stronger the connection becomes). Once that connection has been formed, activation can then spread from "You" to "Good Weather" to "Positive Emotions." When you classically condition yourself with good weather, you can activate positive emotions because of the spreading activation in your target's semantic network.

Well, look at that! We *did* come full circle in the METHODS process. The first chapter explained how our semantic network is our mental framework of the world, and this chapter explained how associations are the building blocks of our semantic network. The profound implications of our semantic network stem beyond the scope of this book, but hopefully you now have a greater appreciation for the nature of associations and how they guide our perception of the world.

## PERSUASION STRATEGY: MAKE FAVORABLE ASSOCIATIONS

In this step of METHODS, you can use associations on a continuous basis to maintain compliance or to add more pressure on your target if she still hasn't complied.

Advertisers constantly take advantage of this principle by associating their brand with appropriate stimuli. For example, they'll often promote their product at sports events to maintain or instill a sense of excitement about their brand. When people feel the excitement from those events, their excitement can transfer to the products in the advertisements and promotional messages.

But besides that obvious strategy of associating your message with positive or relevant stimuli, there are a few other not-so-obvious strategies that you can implement.

**Leverage Metaphors.** You might not realize it, but metaphors are all around us. In fact, some researchers argue that our understanding of the world has largely emerged through seven "deep metaphors" (Zaltman & Zaltman, 2008).

It makes sense if you think about it. If we continuously learn new things by associating those ideas with existing concepts in our semantic network, there had to have been a starting point. In a sense, everything that we come to learn will somehow be tied to the deepest elements of our semantic network, elements that probably relate to primary aspects of survival, such as eating food. And when you stop to reflect on the use of our language, you *do* start to notice an enormous number of those metaphors (Lakoff & Johnson, 1980).

Don't' believe me? Well, I hope that you can at least *swallow* your pride and *stomach* this *meaty* paragraph while I demonstrate. Don't worry, I won't ask you to *regurgitate* this information for an exam; it's purely *food for thought*. And if this *half-baked* idea doesn't convince you, then just let it *digest* and *simmer* for a while; it might start to *eat away* at you. But once you realize the *raw* abundance of these food metaphors, it might seem like a *bittersweet* epiphany. Or if this idea still *smells fishy* and it's not an idea that you can *sink your teeth into*, then I hope you can still *devour* the remaining contents in this book (and I hope it doesn't leave a *sour taste in your mouth*). As long as you don't view this book as just another *flavor of the month*, then I'll be happy, or as I like to say, I'll experience the *sweet smell* of victory.

The use and origin of our language is a fascinating topic that researchers are still trying to understand (and it's far beyond the scope of this book). The main point that I was trying to illustrate is that we come to understand many concepts by relating them to some other concept with which we're more familiar. More importantly, there are a couple persuasion techniques that you can use to take advantage of our innate reliance on metaphors. This section describes two of those techniques.

*Leverage the "Good = Up" Metaphor.* In addition to food, another fundamental metaphor relates to spatial orientations. Vertical positions, in particular, have come to signify the "goodness" of objects. In their cleverly titled article, "Why the Sunny Side Is Up," Brian Meier and Michael Robinson (2004) describe that metaphor:

> Objects that are up or high are often considered to be good, whereas objects that are down or low are often considered to be bad. In the Bible, for example,

> the righteous go "up" to Heaven, whereas sinners
> go "down" to Hell. In the media, movie critics give
> good movies "thumbs up" and bad movies "thumbs
> down.". . . People who smoke marijuana "get high," but
> when the euphoria diminishes, they "come down," and
> happy people feel "up" whereas sad people feel "down."
> (Meier & Robinson, 2004, p. 243)

Because "good" has become associated with people's schema for "up,"
you can enhance the appeal of your message by associating it with
something in an up position.

Suppose that you're purchasing a magazine advertisement, and
the magazine editor mentions that you can choose one of two place-
ments on a particular page: one near the top or one near the bottom.
Though most people typically wouldn't have a preference, you should
choose the location near the top of the page because it would activate
people's "good = up" association, which would generate a more favorable perception of your product and advertisement.

But you don't even need to be an advertiser to take advantage of
this concept. Do you want your kids or spouse to eat healthier? Try
rearranging the refrigerator to put the healthy options near the top
and the unhealthy options near the bottom. That positioning would
help to reinforce a "good = up = healthy" association in your target's
semantic network. It might seem somewhat far-fetched, but research
in marketing shows that in-store products are evaluated more favorably when they are located near the top of the shelves (Chandon et al.,
2009).

*Communicate Using Metaphors.* Given our reliance on metaphors to
understand new concepts, why not use metaphors to communicate
information? As explained, we come to understand new concepts by
relating them to concepts that already exist in our semantic network.
Therefore, you can convey your message more effectively by comparing it to an already existing concept in your target's semantic network.

That notion becomes especially important for abstract ideas and concepts. Experienced marketers consistently convey intangible benefits about their product (e.g., high quality) by comparing it to something tangible because that metaphor helps to "tangiblize" it. For example, Gerald and Lindsay Zaltman (2008) describe how "life insurance companies use ideas associated with various symbols such as umbrellas (Travelers), rocks (Prudential Insurance Company), and hands (Allstate) to convey qualities of protection, sturdiness, and support."

Not only can metaphors help you communicate information more effectively, but they can also enhance the recipient's trust in you. In research that I conducted with a few professors from my good ol' alma mater, we found that if you communicate information by comparing it to something with which a recipient is already familiar, you increase affective trust, a type of trust where the recipient has a strong "gut reaction" to trust you (Kolenda, McGinnis, & Glibkowski, 2012). The takeaway: whenever you need to communicate a new concept to people, you should compare it to something with which they're already familiar.

**Associate with Naturally Occurring Primes.** Here's a quick exercise: mentally list about 5 brands of soda. Did you think of your list? Surprisingly, depending on the time of year that you're reading this book, your list could contain different brands.

In one study, Berger and Fitzsimons (2008) asked people to list some brands of soda and chocolate, and they found that people were more likely to include Reese's in their chocolate list and orange soda (e.g., Sunkist) in their soda list when they were asked that question the day before Halloween. When other people were asked that same question a week later, the frequency of Reese's and orange soda diminished.

Why were those products more popular the day before Halloween? All three concepts—Reese's, Sunkist, and Halloween—share a common linkage: the color orange. People were more likely to include Reese's and Sunkist in their list of brands when they were asked the day before Halloween because the concept of orange was more prevalent in people's minds. Because the concept of orange was more prevalent, those brands popped into their minds more readily through the heightened activation in their semantic network.

Although that may have been a somewhat obvious prime (let's face it, stores *do* tend to blind customers with orange-related products near Halloween), the same researchers conducted a similar study by giving people either an orange or green colored pen to complete a questionnaire. Despite a much more subtle prime, the color of the pen influenced how people evaluated products in the questionnaire. People who were writing with an orange pen significantly preferred orange-related products (e.g., Fanta), whereas people who were using a green pen significantly preferred green products (e.g., Lemon-Lime Gatorade). The subtle exposure to the pen's color triggered conceptual fluency: if someone was primed with an orange-colored pen, the orange-related products appeared in their mind more easily, and that ease of processing became misattributed to a favorable product (and vice versa with the green pen).

Because subtle cues, like the color of a pen, can prime certain concepts, advertisers can take advantage of conceptual fluency by associating their message with common environmental cues that are perceptually similar to their message. Consider the use of *trade characters*—a person, animal, or object that marketers use to symbolize their brand. Many current trade characters are either fictitious (e.g., the Pillsbury Doughboy, the Jolly Green Giant) or rarely seen in a normal day (e.g., Tony the Tiger, Toucan Sam). Rather than choose a fictitious or uncommon trade character, it would be much more effective for advertisers to choose a trade character that people frequently encounter because those "naturally occurring primes" will help consistently remind people of their message.

A more effective strategy can be seen in the E*Trade commercials with the talking babies. Not only does that association subtly imply a positive message about E*Trade (e.g., the service is so easy to use that a baby can use it), but it's also a naturally occurring prime (I'd be willing to bet that you run into babies more frequently than you run into tigers and toucans). In fact, the next time that you see a baby, you might start a conversation with the parents by asking if they've seen "that commercial with the talking baby," which would help spark word-of-mouth for E*Trade.

But perhaps an even better strategy beyond mere trade characters can be found in attaching your message to a naturally occurring need state, such as hunger or thirst. Suppose that an advertiser created a food commercial by using a talking baby. The commercial could take advantage of the common phrase, "food baby" (an expression that refers to someone who just ate a lot of food and looks bloated). The first scene could depict someone feeling hungry, the second scene could show an inside view of that person's stomach and how it's completely empty, and the third scene could show a talking baby on vacation (implying that the person is hungry and doesn't have a "food baby" inside her stomach). It's a pretty absurd example, but it incorporates several psychological principles.

> First, the commercial is so absurd that it's easy to remember (the *bizarreness effect* describes how bizarre images are more easily remembered; McDaniel et al., 1995).
> Second, the next time people experience hunger—a naturally occurring need state—they will be primed to think of your brand. Upon experiencing their hunger, they might remember your silly commercial about the food baby, which would then trigger their memory for your brand.
> Third, the fact that your brand will pop into their mind so easily takes advantage of conceptual fluency; the ease with which your brand came to their mind will be misattributed to a desire to consume your brand (Lee & Labroo, 2004)
> Fourth, since they will already be in a state of need (i.e., hungry), they'll be actively looking for a way to solve that need. Because they will already be thinking of your brand, your food product becomes a perfect candidate to solve their need.

➤ Fifth, the next time that people see a baby (or hear the expression "food baby"), they might ask the people around them if they've seen your commercial, which would spark a conversation around your brand (Berger, 2013). These conversations would sustain ongoing word-of-mouth with your brand and automate part of your marketing efforts.

Although this strategy has the most relevance for marketers, the principle is very powerful. To keep your product or message at the top of someone's mind, you should associate it with something that people encounter on a frequent basis. Each time someone is exposed to those "naturally occurring primes," they will likely think of your product or message.

**Enhance Your Attractiveness.** Welcome to the last specific strategy in the book. I decided to end with a topic that: (1) packs a powerful persuasion punch, and (2) remains in high demand. In this strategy, you'll learn how to enhance your perceived attractiveness.

Imagine that a researcher approached you while you were walking across a sturdy bridge, and she asked you to complete a questionnaire. Would your perception of her attractiveness change if, instead of a safe bridge, you were walking across a wobbly suspension bridge? Research suggests that it *would* change because of your heightened arousal (ah yes, the same state of arousal that was discussed a few chapters ago).

Dutton and Aron (1974) conducted that bridge experiment to examine the connection between arousal and attraction. In their study, a female approached males when they were walking across either a wobbly suspension bridge or a safe and sturdy bridge. After each male completed the questionnaire, the female researcher gave him her phone number and invited him to call with any questions. The results were astounding. Of the sixteen males who crossed the safe bridge, only two of them (13 percent) followed up with a phone call. Of the 18 males that crossed the wobbly suspension bridge, however, a whopping 9 of them (50 percent) called the female researcher.

The dangerous nature of the suspension bridge caused those males to experience higher arousal (e.g., rapid heartbeat, heavy breathing, etc.), and they looked for surrounding cues to label that aroused state. Although the bridge served as one possible explanation, the female researcher represented another possible explanation. Because males who crossed the safe bridge experienced very little arousal, there was nothing to misattribute to the female researcher, and so fewer of those males followed up with a phone call.

Other studies have even found that people can remain fully aware of the true source of arousal yet still develop stronger feelings of attraction toward the other person. You're reclining back in a dentist's chair when *bam*! The chair suddenly drops back 35-degrees, and a heavy brass plate collides with a steel plate on the floor, producing an incredibly loud and startling bang. Unless you're Superman, you'd probably feel some arousal from that startling experience, as did participants in one study (Dienstbier, 1989). But even though participants knew the true source of their arousal, they still found the experimenter nearby to be significantly more attractive.

How can you take advantage of this principle to enhance your perceived attractiveness? Fortunately, there are plenty of situations where people experience a naturally higher state of arousal besides a wobbly bridge and a broken dentist's chair. If you're hoping to meet a potential romantic partner, one option is to join a gym, a place where nearly everyone is in a natural state of arousal. When you interact with fellow gym goers, they're more likely to interpret their state of arousal as attractive feelings toward you, and thus you stand a better chance of sparking a romance with gym members (White, Fishbein, & Rutsein, 1981).

Similarly, if you begin dating someone, you could choose dates that take advantage of naturally occurring arousal, such as a scary movie or an amusement park. Scary movies have been found to increase the affiliation between couples (Cohen, Waugh, & Place, 1989), and roller coasters at amusement parks lead people to rate their seat partner as more attractive (Meston & Frohlich, 2003).

There are other options out there too; you just need to use some creative brainstorming. Like every principle in this book, you're not limited to the example strategies that I described in the chapter. As I mentioned in the introduction, I chose to explain the psychology behind every principle so that you can brainstorm your own persuasion applications. Rather than give you fish, my goal has been to teach you how to catch your own fish.

Now that you understand some of the principles that guide human behavior, you can start to develop your own creative uses for those principles. I'm confident that you'll soon find that the applications are truly endless. Much like a puppeteer can use the strings to control a marionette, you'll soon find yourself becoming a master puppeteer in our world full of human marionettes. And with that last "metaphor" (wink wink), I'll now present one last Real World Application and end the book with a unique summary to help you make sense of all of the principles that were described throughout the book.

# REAL WORLD APPLICATION:
# THE FAMILY VACATION (PART 3)

You've somewhat cracked your husband's closed-mindedness, and he's now on the fence about taking the family trip to Disneyland. To give him that extra boost of persuasion, you decide to classically condition him to find the vacation even more appealing.

Each time that your husband is in a good mood, you bring up the idea of travel in general. You don't bring up the idea about the family vacation (because that might spark psychological reactance if he notices your devious motive). Instead, you mention unrelated aspects of travel, such as your coworker's recent trip to France or your family's trip to Italy a few years ago.

Not only does that tactic further reinforce your repeated exposures, but it also classically conditions your husband to find the idea of travel more appealing. By consistently presenting the idea of travel to your husband when he's in a pleasant mood, you can cause his positive emotions to transfer to the family vacation idea. Your husband will unknowingly develop a more positive attitude toward the vacation because of those continuous exposures.

After you condition him for a week or two, you once again mention the possible family trip to Disneyland, and his response is a breath of fresh air. He's finally on board. Overjoyed, you give him a big hug and kiss as your mind frantically races about planning the trip. You can't wait to give your daughter a memory that will last a lifetime.

# Putting It All Together

So there you go. That was *Methods of Persuasion*. You can smile knowing that we officially reached the end of the book.

Before I **summarize** the main principles from the book, it's now my turn to try and persuade you to comply with a request. I'm at a huge disadvantage, though, because you're now familiar with all of my potential tactics; if I incorporate any of the strategies from the book, you'll see right through them. So I'm forced to rely on one final persuasion technique: a genuine, heartfelt plea.

What's the favor? I need you to purchase 100 copies of this book to give to your friends so that you can spread the word about my book . . . I'm kidding! The favor is pretty small. And, in fact, I'll even let you choose between one of two potential options (or if you want to do both, then that's even better!). If you thought that the information in this book was interesting and/or helpful, you could help me out *tremendously* if you:

> ➤ Write a positive review on Amazon (which will help me market the book through social proof).
> ➤ Subscribe to my blog at www.NickKolenda.com (which will help you stay updated on new articles, books, and videos from me).

So, in regard to not using psychological principles in my request . . . I might have used a few principles. Well, I might have used more than a few. Did you realize that I used over half the principles from this book in that short request? Let's backtrack and review the principles that I used so that you have a better idea about how you can start implementing them in your own life. This review will be a good summary of the book.

The psychology started in the very first paragraph when I mentioned that you can smile having reached the end of the book. Using the word "smile" was two-fold. First, exposing people to the word "smile" activates the facial muscles used in smiling (Foroni & Semin, 2009), so that was my attempt to control your body language (Chapter 4). Second, people generally put "smiling" in their schema of open-mindedness, so exposing you to that word may have primed a perception that was more open-minded (Chapter 1).

Further, you'll notice that I specifically said that you can smile knowing that "we" officially reached the end of the book. Using that first person pronoun helped emphasize that we belong to the same ingroup (Chapter 7) because it subtly implied that we were part of the same arduous journey, so to speak.

In the next paragraph, you might have noticed that "summarize" was bolded, which probably seemed out of place. This deliberate bolding was my attempt to grab your attention using the pique technique. If you were mindlessly reading along, that "mistake" may have woken you up from reading on autopilot so that you would use systematic processing to evaluate my request (Chapter 10).

As that same paragraph continues, I tried to disguise my psychological strategies by saying that it was pointless to try to use them. By disguising my strategies, I tried to make it seem like I wasn't trying to persuade you or control your behavior; otherwise, you may have engaged in psychological reactance by automatically resisting my request (Chapter 13).

Immediately before I presented my request in the next paragraph, I anchored your perception by using a contrast effect. The request to purchase 100 copies of my book seemed so large that when I later presented the two smaller requests, you perceived them to be even smaller than if I hadn't presented that large request (Chapter 2).

Even the two requests themselves contained psychological principles. Not only did I promote your autonomy by giving you the choice of the request (Chapter 12), but I also followed each request with justification. If you were still using heuristic processing (which we all do to some extent), you would automatically assume that those reasons would be valid, and you would be more likely to comply (Chapter 11).

It's amazing how easy it can be to implement those principles into everyday situations. In one simple request to you, I managed to use a principle from over half of the chapters in this book. Further, even though you were aware of those principles, I'm willing to bet that many of them still flew under your radar. That's another great benefit about these principles. When you implement them on people who don't know them, they'll be even more invisible. Finally, I hope you also realize that, although this book outlines a step-by-step process, you can also pick and choose when to use these principles. The METHODS process is a helpful guide, but there are no strict step-by-step rules. You're free to use the principles at your disposal.

With all applications aside, however, you could truly help me out by doing one of those two options that I mentioned. If you didn't think this book merited one of those two options, then please let me know what it *would* need. I poured my heart and brain into making this book as interesting and helpful as possible, so if you can think of a way to improve it, I would love to incorporate that suggestion into the next edition.

Lastly, Future Nick inserted this final paragraph to let you know that I published a new book in 2019. It's called *The Tangled Mind*. In that book, you'll learn even more factors that subtly influence your perception and behavior.

# References

Aarts, H., & Dijksterhuis, A. (2003). The silence of the library: Environment, situational norm, and social behavior. *Journal of Personality and Social Psychology, 84*(1), 18–28.

Alter, A. L., & Oppenheimer, D. M. (2006). Predicting short-term stock fluctuations by using processing fluency. *Proceedings of the National Academy of Sciences, 103*(24), 9369–9372.

Alter, A. L., & Oppenheimer, D. M. (2009). Uniting the tribes of fluency to form a metacognitive nation. *Personality and Social Psychology Review, 13*(3), 219–235.

Anderson, C. A., & Bushman, B. J. (2001). Effects of violent video games on aggressive behavior, aggressive cognition, aggressive affect, physiological arousal, and prosocial behavior: A meta-analytic review of the scientific literature. *Psychological Science, 12*(5), 353–359.

Ariely, D. (2009). *Predictably Irrational: The Hidden Forces that Shape our Decisions.* New York: HarperCollins.

Ariely, D., Gneezy, U., Loewenstein, G., & Mazar, N. (2009). Large stakes and big mistakes. *The Review of Economic Studies, 76*(2), 451–469.

Aronson, E., & Carlsmith, J. M. (1963). Effect of the severity of threat on the devaluation of forbidden behavior. *The Journal of Abnormal and Social Psychology, 66*(6), 584.

Asch, S. (1946). Forming impressions of personality. *Journal of Abnormal Psychology, 41*, 258.

Asch, S. (1951). Effects of group pressure upon the modification and distortion of judgments. *Groups, Leadership, and Men. S*, 222–236.

Baeyens, F., Eelen, P., Crombez, G., & Van den Bergh, O. (1992). Human evaluative conditioning: Acquisition trials, presentation schedule, evaluative style and contingency awareness. *Behaviour Research and Therapy, 30*(2), 133–142.

Bargh, J. A., Chen, M., & Burrows, L. (1996). Automaticity of social behavior: Direct effects of trait construct and stereotype activation on action. *Journal of Personality and Social Psychology, 71*(2), 230–244.

Berger, J. (2013). *Contagious: Why Things Catch On*. New York: Simon & Schuster.

Berger, J., & Fitzsimons, G. (2008). Dogs on the street, pumas on your feet: How cues in the environment influence product evaluation and choice. *Journal of Marketing Research, 45*(1), 1–14.

Bem, D. J. (1972). Self-Perception Theory. *Advances in Experimental Social Psychology, 6*, 1–62.

Bless, H., Bohner, G., Schwarz, N., & Strack, F. (1990). Mood and persuasion: A cognitive response analysis. *Personality and Social Psychology Bulletin, 16*(2), 331–345.

Bornstein, R. F., Leone, D. R., & Galley, D. J. (1987). The generalizability of subliminal mere exposure effects: Influence of stimuli perceived without awareness on social behavior. *Journal of Personality and Social Psychology, 53*(6), 1070–1079.

Bransford, J. D., & Johnson, M. K. (1972). Contextual prerequisites for understanding: Some investigations of comprehension and recall. *Journal of Verbal Learning and Verbal Behavior, 11*(6), 717–726.

Brehm, J. W. (1966). *Response to loss of freedom: A theory of psychological reactance*. New York: Academic Press.

Brendl, C. M., Chattopadhyay, A., Pelham, B. W., & Carvallo, M. (2005). Name letter branding: Valence transfers when product specific needs are active. *Journal of Consumer Research, 32*(3), 405–415.

Briñol, P., & Petty, R. E. (2008). Embodied persuasion: Fundamental processes by which bodily responses can impact attitudes. *Embodiment Grounding: Social, Cognitive, Affective, and Neuroscientific Approaches*, 184–207.

Brock, T. C. (1968). Implications of commodity theory for value change. *Psychological Foundations of Attitudes*, 243–275.

Bull, P. E. (1987). *Posture and Gesture* (Vol. 16). Oxford: Pergamon Press.

Burger, J. M., Horita, M., Kinoshita, L., Roberts, K., & Vera, C. (1997). Effects on time on the norm of reciprocity. *Basic and Applied Social Psychology, 19*(1), 91–100.

Burger, J. M., Messian, N., Patel, S., del Prado, A., & Anderson, C. (2004). What a coincidence! The effects of incidental similarity on compliance. *Personality and Social Psychology Bulletin, 30*(1), 35–43.

Burger, J. M., Sanchez, J., Imberi, J. E., & Grande, L. R. (2009). The norm of reciprocity as an internalized social norm: Returning favors even when no one finds out. *Social Influence, 4*(1), 11–17.

Burnkrant, R. E., & Unnava, H. R. (1995). Effects of self-referencing on persuasion. *Journal of Consumer Research*, 22(1), 17–26.

Bushman, B. J., & Stack, A. D. (1996). Forbidden fruit versus tainted fruit: Effects of warning labels on attraction to television violence. *Journal of Experimental Psychology: Applied, 2*(3), 207–226.

Carlin, A. S., Hoffman, H. G., & Weghorst, S. (1997). Virtual reality and tactile augmentation in the treatment of spider phobia: a case report. *Behaviour Research and Therapy, 35*(2), 153–158.

Catherall, D. R. (2004). *Handbook of Stress, Trauma, and the Family* (Vol. 10). New York: Brunner-Routledge.

Chaiken, S. (1980). Heuristic versus systematic information processing and the use of source versus message cues in persuasion. *Journal of Personality and Social Psychology, 39*(5), 752–766.

Chandon, P., Hutchinson, J. W., Bradlow, E. T., & Young, S. H. (2009). Does in-store marketing work? Effects of the number and position of shelf facings on brand attention and evaluation at the point of purchase. *Journal of Marketing, 73*, 1–17.

Chartrand, T. L., Dalton, A. N., & Fitzsimons, G. J. (2007). Nonconscious relationship reactance: When significant others prime opposing goals. *Journal of Experimental Social Psychology, 43*(5), 719–726.

Chatterjee, A. (2010). Neuroaesthetics: A coming of age story. *Journal of Cognitive Neuroscience, 23*(1), 53–62.

Chernev, A. (2011). Semantic anchoring in sequential evaluations of vices and virtues. *Journal of Consumer Research, 37*(5), 761–774.

Cialdini, R. B. (2001). *Influence: Science and Practice.* Boston: Allyn & Bacon.

Cialdini, R. B. (2003). Crafting normative messages to protect the environment. *Current Directions in Psychological Science, 12*(4), 105–109.

Cialdini, R. B., Demaine, L. J., Sagarin, B. J., Barrett, D. W., Rhoads, K., & Winter, P. L. (2006). Managing social norms for persuasive impact. *Social Influence, 1*(1), 3–15.

Cialdini, R. B., Reno, R. R., & Kallgren, C. A. (1990). A focus theory of normative conduct: Recycling the concept of norms to reduce littering in public places. *Journal of Personality and Social Psychology, 58*(6), 1015–1026.

Cialdini, R. B., Vincent, J. E., Lewis, S. K., Catalan, J., Wheeler, D., & Darby, B. L. (1975). Reciprocal concessions procedure for inducing compliance: The door-in-the-face technique. *Journal of Personality and Social Psychology, 31*(2), 206–215.

Cohen, B., Waugh, G., & Place, K. (1989). At the movies: An unobtrusive study of arousal-attraction. *The Journal of Social Psychology, 129*(5), 691–693.

Collins, A. M., & Loftus, E. F. (1975). A spreading-activation theory of semantic processing. *Psychological Review, 82*(6), 407–428.

DeBono, K. G., & Krim, S. (1997). Compliments and perceptions of product quality: An individual difference perspective. *Journal of Applied Social Psychology, 27*(15), 1359–1366.

Deci, E. L., & Ryan, R. M. (1980). The empirical exploration of intrinsic motivational processes. *Advances in Experimental Social Psychology, 13*(2), 39–80.

Deighton, J., Romer, D., & McQueen, J. (1989). Using drama to persuade. *Journal of Consumer Research,* 335–343.

DeWall, C. N., MacDonald, G., Webster, G. D., Masten, C. L., Baumeister, R. F., Powell, C., Combs, D., Schurtz, D., Stillman, T., Tice,

D., & Eisenberger, N. I. (2010). Acetaminophen reduces social pain behavioral and neural evidence. *Psychological Science, 21*(7), 931–937.

Diehl, K., & Lamberton, C. (2008). Great expectations?! Assortment size, expectations and satisfaction. *Journal of Marketing Research, 47*(2), 312–322.

Dienstbier, R. A. (1989). Arousal and physiological toughness: implications for mental and physical health. *Psychological Review, 96*(1), 84.

Dijksterhuis, A., & van Knippenberg, A. (1998). The relation between perception and behavior, or how to win a game of Trivial Pursuit. *Journal of Personality and Social Psychology, 74*(4), 865.

Drolet, A. L., & Morris, M. W. (2000). Rapport in conflict resolution: Accounting for how face-to-face contact fosters mutual cooperation in mixed-motive conflicts. *Journal of Experimental Social Psychology, 36*(1), 26–50.

Dutton, D. G., & Aron, A. P. (1974). Some evidence for heightened sexual attraction under conditions of high anxiety. *Journal of Personality and Social Psychology, 30*(4), 510.

Dunyon, J., Gossling, V., Willden, S., & Seiter, J. S. (2010). Compliments and purchasing behavior in telephone sales interactions. *Psychological Reports, 106*(1), 27.

Eisenberger, N. I., & Lieberman, M. D. (2004). Why rejection hurts: a common neural alarm system for physical and social pain. *Trends in Cognitive Sciences, 8*(7), 294–300.

Englich, B., Mussweiler, T., & Strack, F. (2006). Playing dice with criminal sentences: The influence of irrelevant anchors on experts' judicial decision making. *Personality and Social Psychology Bulletin, 32*(2), 188–200.

Epley, N., & Gilovich, T. (2006). The anchoring-and-adjustment heuristic: Why the adjustments are insufficient. *Psychological Science, 17*(4), 311–318.

Epley, N., & Whitchurch, E. (2008). Mirror, mirror on the wall: Enhancement in self-recognition. *Personality and Social Psychology Bulletin, 34*(9), 1159–1170.

Falk, A., & Kosfeld, M. (2006). The hidden costs of control. *The American Economic Review*, 1611–1630.

Festinger, L., & Carlsmith, J. M. (1959). Cognitive consequences of forced compliance. *The Journal of Abnormal and Social Psychology*, *58*(2), 203.

Fitzsimons, G. M., & Bargh, J. A. (2003). Thinking of you: Nonconscious pursuit of interpersonal goals associated with relationship partners. *Journal of Personality and Social Psychology*, *84*(1), 148.

Fitzsimons, G. M., Chartrand, T. L., & Fitzsimons, G. J. (2008). Automatic effects of brand exposure on motivated behavior: how apple makes you "think different." *Journal of Consumer Research*, *35*(1), 21–35.

Foroni, F., & Semin, G. R. (2009). Language that puts you in touch with your bodily feelings: The multimodal responsiveness of affective expressions. *Psychological Science*, *20*(8), 974–980.

Förster, J. (2003). The influence of approach and avoidance motor actions on food intake. *European Journal of Social Psychology*, *33*(3), 339–350.

Freedman, J. L., & Fraser, S. C. (1966). Compliance without pressure: The foot-in-the-door technique. *Journal of Personality and Social Psychology*, *4*(2), 195–202.

Friedman, R., & Elliot, A. J. (2008). The effect of arm crossing on persistence and performance. *European Journal of Social Psychology*, *38*(3), 449–461.

Frieze, I. H., Olson, J. E., & Russell, J. (1991). Attractiveness and income for men and women in management. *Journal of Applied Social Psychology*, *21*(13), 1039–1057.

Gandhi, B., & Oakley, D. A. (2005). Does 'hypnosis' by any other name smell as sweet? The efficacy of 'hypnotic' inductions depends on the label 'hypnosis.' *Consciousness and Cognition*, *14*(2), 304–315.

Gawronski, B., Bodenhausen, G. V., & Becker, A. P. (2007). I like it, because I like myself: Associative self-anchoring and post-decisional change of implicit evaluations. *Journal of Experimental Social Psychology*, *43*(2), 221–232.

Glocker, M. L., Langleben, D. D., Ruparel, K., Loughead, J. W., Gur, R. C., & Sachser, N. (2009). Baby schema in infant faces induces cuteness perception and motivation for caretaking in adults. *Ethology, 115*(3), 257–263.

Gneezy, U., Meier, S., & Rey-Biel, P. (2011). When and why incentives (don't) work to modify behavior. *The Journal of Economic Perspectives, 25*(4), 191–209.

Gneezy, U., & Rustichini, A. (2000a). Pay enough or don't pay at all. *The Quarterly Journal of Economics, 115*(3), 791–810.

Gneezy, U., & Rustichini, A. (2000b). A Fine is a Price. *The Journal of Legal Studies, 29*(1), 1–17.

Goldsmith, K., Cho, E. K., & Dhar, R. (2012). When guilt begets pleasure: The positive effect of a negative emotion. *Journal of Marketing Research, 49*(6), 872–881.

Goldstein, N. J., & Cialdini, R. B. (2007). The spyglass self: A model of vicarious self-perception. *Journal of Personality and Social Psychology, 92*(3), 402.

Goldstein, N. J., Cialdini, R. B., & Griskevicius, V. (2008). A room with a viewpoint: Using social norms to motivate environmental conservation in hotels. *Journal of Consumer Research, 35*(3), 472–482.

Guéguen, N. (2009). Mimicry and seduction: An evaluation in a courtship context. *Social Influence, 4*(4), 249–255.

Guéguen, N., Martin, A., & Meineri, S. (2011). Mimicry and helping behavior: an evaluation of mimicry on explicit helping request. *The Journal of Social Psychology, 151*(1), 1–4.

Harmon-Jones, E. (2000). Cognitive dissonance and experienced negative affect: Evidence that dissonance increases experienced negative affect even in the absence of aversive consequences. *Personality and Social Psychology Bulletin, 26*(12), 1490–1501.

Hassin, R. R. (2008). Being open minded without knowing why: Evidence from nonconscious goal pursuit. *Social Cognition, 26*(5), 578–592.

Hildum, D. C., & Brown, R. W. (1956). Verbal reinforcement and interviewer bias. *Journal of Abnormal Psychology, 53*(1), 108.

Holland, R. W., Hendriks, M., & Aarts, H. (2005). Smells like clean spirit: Nonconscious effects of scent on cognition and behavior. *Psychological Science, 16*(9), 689–693.

Holland, R. W., Wennekers, A. M., Bijlstra, G., Jongenelen, M. M., & Van Knippenberg, A. (2009). Self-symbols as implicit motivators. *Social Cognition, 27*(4), 579–600.

Houlfort, N., Koestner, R., Joussemet, M., Nantel-Vivier, A., & Lekes, N. (2002). The impact of performance-contingent rewards on perceived autonomy and competence. *Motivation and Emotion, 26*(4), 279–295.

Howard, D. J. (1990). The influence of verbal responses to common greetings on compliance behavior: The foot-in-the-mouth effect. *Journal of Applied Social Psychology, 20*(14), 1185–1196.

Huang, L., Galinsky, A. D., Gruenfeld, D. H., & Guillory, L. E. (2011). Powerful postures versus powerful roles: Which is the proximate correlate of thought and behavior? *Psychological Science, 22*(1), 95–102.

Huber, J., Payne, J. W., & Puto, C. (1982). Adding asymmetrically dominated alternatives: Violations of regularity and the similarity hypothesis. *Journal of Consumer Research*, 90–98.

I wonder if anyone actually reads these references. If you happened to stumble upon this hidden message, then pat yourself on the back. There's some really cool research here that you might find very helpful.

Iyengar, S. S., Huberman, G., & Jiang, W. (2004). How much choice is too much? Contributions to 401 (k) retirement plans. *Pension Design and Structure: New Lessons from Behavioral Finance*, 83–96.

Jacob, C., Guéguen, N., Martin, A., & Boulbry, G. (2011). Retail salespeople's mimicry of customers: Effects on consumer behavior. *Journal of Retailing and Consumer Services, 18*(5), 381–388.

Jones, M. C. (1924). The elimination of children's fears. *Journal of Experimental Psychology, 7*(5), 382.

Jones, C. R., Olson, M. A., & Fazio, R. H. (2010). Evaluative conditioning: The "how" question. *Advances in Experimental Social Psychology, 43*, 205–255.

Jostmann, N. B., Lakens, D., & Schubert, T. W. (2009). Weight as an embodiment of importance. *Psychological Science, 20*(9), 1169–1174.

Kawabata, H., & Zeki, S. (2004). Neural correlates of beauty. *Journal of Neurophysiology, 91*(4), 1699–1705.

Kenrick, D. T., Gutierres, S. E., & Goldberg, L. L. (1989). Influence of popular erotica on judgments of strangers and mates. *Journal of Experimental Social Psychology, 25*(2), 159–167.

Koenigs, M., & Tranel, D. (2008). Prefrontal cortex damage abolishes brand-cued changes in cola preference. *Social Cognitive and Affective Neuroscience, 3*(1), 1–6.

Kolenda N, McGinnis L, Glibkowski B. (2012). Knowledge transfer antecedents and consequences: A conceptual model. Working paper.

Krosnick, J. A., Betz, A. L., Jussim, L. J., Lynn, A. R., & Stephens, L. (1992). Subliminal conditioning of attitudes. *Personality and Social Psychology Bulletin, 18*(2), 152–162.

Kühn, S., Müller, B. C., van Baaren, R. B., Wietzker, A., Dijksterhuis, A., & Brass, M. (2010). Why do I like you when you behave like me? Neural mechanisms mediating positive consequences of observing someone being imitated. *Social Neuroscience, 5*(4), 384–392.

Lakin, J. L., Jefferis, V. E., Cheng, C. M., & Chartrand, T. L. (2003). The chameleon effect as social glue: Evidence for the evolutionary significance of nonconscious mimicry. *Journal of Nonverbal Behavior, 27*(3), 145–162.

Lakoff, G., & Johnson, M. (1980). The metaphorical structure of the human conceptual system. *Cognitive Science, 4*(2), 195–208.

Langer, E., Blank, A., & Chanowitz, B. (1978). The mindlessness of ostensibly thoughtful action: The role of "placebic" information in interpersonal interaction. *Journal of Personality and Social Psychology, 36*(6), 635–642.

Latané, B., & Darley, J. M. (1968). Group inhibition of bystander intervention in emergencies. *Journal of Personality and Social Psychology, 10*(3), 215–221.

Lee, L., Frederick, S., & Ariely, D. (2006). Try it, you'll like it: The influence of expectation, consumption, and revelation on preferences for beer. *Psychological Science, 17*(12), 1054–1058.

Lee, A. Y., & Labroo, A. A. (2004). The effect of conceptual and perceptual fluency on brand evaluation. *Journal of Marketing Research*, 151–165.

Leippe, M. R., & Eisenstadt, D. (1994). Generalization of dissonance reduction: Decreasing prejudice through induced compliance. *Journal of Personality and Social Psychology, 67*(3), 395–413.

Lindgaard, G., Fernandes, G., Dudek, C., & Brown, J. (2006). Attention web designers: You have 50 milliseconds to make a good first impression! *Behaviour & Information Technology, 25*(2), 115–126.

Lynn, M., & McCall, M. (2009). Techniques for increasing servers' tips: How generalizable are they? *Cornell Hospitality Quarterly, 50*(2), 198–208.

MacInnis, D. J., Moorman, C., & Jaworski, B. J. (1991). Enhancing and measuring consumers' motivation, opportunity, and ability to process brand information from ads. *Journal of Marketing*, 32–53.

Mackie, D. M., & Worth, L. T. (1991). Feeling good, but not thinking straight: The impact of positive mood on persuasion. *Emotion and Social Judgments, 23*, 210–219.

Macrae, C. N., & Johnston, L. (1998). Help, I need somebody: Automatic action and inaction. *Social Cognition, 16*(4), 400–417.

Madey, S. F., Simo, M., Dillworth, D., Kemper, D., Toczynski, A., & Perella, A. (1996). They do get more attractive at closing time, but only when you are not in a relationship. *Basic and Applied Social Psychology, 18*(4), 387–393.

Martin, P. Y., Hamilton, V. E., McKimmie, B. M., Terry, D. J., & Martin, R. (2007). Effects of caffeine on persuasion and attitude change: The role of secondary tasks in manipulating systematic message processing. *European Journal of Social Psychology, 37*(2), 320–338.

McClure, S. M., Li, J., Tomlin, D., Cypert, K. S., Montague, L. M., & Montague, P. R. (2004). Neural correlates of behavioral preference for culturally familiar drinks. *Neuron, 44*(2), 379–387.

McDaniel, M. A., Einstein, G. O., DeLosh, E. L., May, C. P., & Brady, P. (1995). The bizarreness effect: It's not surprising, it's complex. *Journal of Experimental Psychology. Learning, Memory, and Cognition, 21*(2), 422.

McFerran, B., Dahl, D. W., Fitzsimons, G. J., & Morales, A. C. (2010a). Might an overweight waitress make you eat more? How the body type of others is sufficient to alter our food consumption. *Journal of Consumer Psychology, 20*(2), 146.

McFerran, B., Dahl, D. W., Fitzsimons, G. J., & Morales, A. C. (2010b). I'll have what she's having: Effects of social influence and body type on the food choices of others. *Journal of Consumer Research, 36*(6), 915–929.

McGuire, W. J. (1964). Inducing resistance to persuasion: Some contemporary approaches. *Advances in Experimental Social Psychology, 1*, 192–229.

Meier, B. P., & Robinson, M. D. (2004). Why the sunny side is up: Associations between affect and vertical position. *Psychological Science, 15*(4), 243–247.

Meston, C. M., & Frohlich, P. F. (2003). Love at first fright: Partner salience moderates roller-coaster-induced excitation transfer. *Archives of Sexual Behavior, 32*(6), 537–544.

Milgram, S. (1973). Behavioral study of obedience. *Journal of Abnormal and Social Psychology, 67*(4), 371–378.

Miller, G. (1956). The magical number seven, plus or minus two: Some limits on our capacity for processing information. *The Psychological Review, 63*, 81–97.

Miller, N., & Campbell, D. T. (1959). Recency and primacy in persuasion as a function of the timing of speeches and measurements. *Journal of Abnormal Psychology, 59*(1), 1.

Mita, T. H., Dermer, M., & Knight, J. (1977). Reversed facial images and the mere-exposure hypothesis. *Journal of Personality and Social Psychology, 35*(8), 597–601.

Mogilner, C., Rudnick, T., & Iyengar, S. S. (2008). The mere categorization effect: How the presence of categories increases choosers' perceptions of assortment variety and outcome satisfaction. *Journal of Consumer Research, 35*(2), 202–215.

Monahan, J. L., Murphy, S. T., & Zajonc, R. B. (2000). Subliminal mere exposure: Specific, general, and diffuse effects. *Psychological Science, 11*(6), 462–466.

Montoya, R. M., Horton, R. S., & Kirchner, J. (2008). Is actual similarity necessary for attraction? A meta-analysis of actual and perceived similarity. *Journal of Social and Personal Relationships, 25*(6), 889–922.

Morales, A. C., & Fitzsimons, G. J. (2007). Product contagion: Changing consumer evaluations through physical contact with "disgusting" products. *Journal of Marketing Research*, 272–283.

Moreland, R. L., & Beach, S. R. (1992). Exposure effects in the classroom: The development of affinity among students. *Journal of Experimental Social Psychology, 28*(3), 255–276.

Murdock Jr., B. B. (1962). The serial position effect of free recall. *Journal of Experimental Psychology, 64*(5), 482.

Mussweiler, T., & Strack, F. (2000). Numeric judgments under uncertainty: The role of knowledge in anchoring. *Journal of Experimental Social Psychology, 36*(5), 495–518.

Nedungadi, P. (1990). Recall and consumer consideration sets: Influencing choice without altering brand evaluations. *Journal of Consumer Research*, 263–276.

Nickerson, R. S. (1998). Confirmation bias: A ubiquitous phenomenon in many guises. *Review of General Psychology, 2*(2), 175.

Niedenthal, P. M., Barsalou, L. W., Winkielman, P., Krauth-Gruber, S., & Ric, F. (2005). Embodiment in attitudes, social perception, and emotion. *Personality and Social Psychology Review, 9*(3), 184–211.

Nuttin, J. M. (1985). Narcissism beyond gestalt and awareness: The name letter effect. *European Journal of Social Psychology, 15*(3), 353–361.

Ono, H. (1967). Difference threshold for stimulus length under simultaneous and nonsimultaneous viewing conditions. *Perception & Psychophysics, 2*(5), 201–207.

Parker, J. R., & Lehmann, D. R. (2011). When shelf-based scarcity impacts consumer preferences. *Journal of Retailing, 87*(2), 142–155.

Patall, E. A., Cooper, H., & Wynn, S. R. (2010). The effectiveness and relative importance of choice in the classroom. *Journal of Educational Psychology, 102*(4), 896.

Pelham, B. W., Carvallo, M., & Jones, J. T. (2005). Implicit egotism. *Current Directions in Psychological Science, 14*(2), 106–110.

Pelham, B. W., Mirenberg, M. C., & Jones, J. T. (2002). Why Susie sells seashells by the seashore: Implicit egotism and major life decisions. *Journal of Personality and Social Psychology, 82*(4), 469–487.

Pepitone, A., & DiNubile, M. (1976). Contrast effects in judgments of crime severity and the punishment of criminal violators. *Journal of Personality and Social Psychology, 33*(4), 448.

Perdue, C. W., Dovidio, J. F., Gurtman, M. B., & Tyler, R. B. (1990). Us and them: Social categorization and the process of intergroup bias. *Journal of Personality and Social Psychology, 59*(3), 475–486.

Petty, R. E., & Cacioppo, J. T. (1984). Source factors and the elaboration likelihood model of persuasion. *Advances in Consumer Research, 11*(1), 668–672.

Petty, R. E., & Cacioppo, J. T. (1986). The elaboration likelihood model of persuasion. In L. Berkowitz (Ed.) *Advances in Experimental Social Psychology* (Vol. 19, pp. 121–203) New York: Academic Press.

Petty, R. E., & Cacioppo, J. T. (1990). Involvement and persuasion: Tradition versus integration. *Psychological Bulletin, 107*(3), 367–374.

Petty, R. E., Cacioppo, J. T., & Heesacker, M. (1981). Effects of rhetorical questions on persuasion: A cognitive response analysis. *Journal of Personality and Social Psychology, 40*(3), 432–440.

Plassmann, H., O'Doherty, J., Shiv, B., & Rangel, A. (2008). Marketing actions can modulate neural representations of experienced pleasantness. *Proceedings of the National Academy of Sciences, 105*(3), 1050–1054.

Pocheptsova, A., Labroo, A. A., & Dhar, R. (2010). Making products feel special: When metacognitive difficulty enhances evaluation. *Journal of Marketing Research, 47*(6), 1059–1069.

Quattrone, G. A., Lawrence, C. P., Finkel, S. E., & Andrus, D. C. (1984). Explorations in anchoring: The effects of prior range, anchor extremity, and suggestive hints. Unpublished Manuscript, Stanford University.

Reber, R., Schwarz, N., & Winkielman, P. (2004). Processing fluency and aesthetic pleasure: Is beauty in the perceiver's processing experience?. *Personality and Social Psychology Review, 8*(4), 364–382.

Rhodes, G., Simmons, L. W., & Peters, M. (2005). Attractiveness and sexual behavior: Does attractiveness enhance mating success? *Evolution and Human Behavior, 26*(2), 186–201.

Rogers, R. W., & Mewborn, C. R. (1976). Fear appeals and attitude change: effects of a threat's noxiousness, probability of occurrence, and the efficacy of coping responses. *Journal of Personality and Social Psychology, 34*(1), 54–61.

Rist, R. C. (1970). Student social class and teacher expectations: The self-fulfilling prophecy in ghetto education. *Harvard Educational Review, 40*(3), 411–451.

Rucker, D. D., Petty, R. E., & Briñol, P. (2008). What's in a frame anyway?: A meta-cognitive analysis of the impact of one versus two sided message framing on attitude certainty. *Journal of Consumer Psychology, 18*, 137–149.

Ryan, R. M. (1982). Control and information in the intrapersonal sphere: An extension of cognitive evaluation theory. *Journal of Personality and Social Psychology, 43*(3), 450–461.

Sanbonmatsu, D. M., & Kardes, F. R. (1988). The effects of physiological arousal on information processing and persuasion. *Journal of Consumer Research*, 379–385.

Santos, M. D., Leve, C., & Pratkanis, A. R. (1994). Hey buddy, can you spare seventeen cents? Mindful persuasion and the pique technique. *Journal of Applied Social Psychology, 24*(9), 755–764.

Schachter, S., & Singer, J. E. (1962). Cognitive, social, and physiological determinants of emotional state. *Psychological Review, 69*(5), 379–399.

Schubert, T. W., & Koole, S. L. (2009). The embodied self: Making a fist enhances men's power-related self-conceptions. *Journal of Experimental Social Psychology, 45*(4), 828–834.

Schwartz, B. (2004). *The Paradox of Choice: Why Less is More.* New York: Ecco.

Schwarz, N., Bless, H., Strack, F., Klumpp, G., Rittenauer-Schatka, H., & Simons, A. (1991). Ease of retrieval as information: Another look at the availability heuristic. *Journal of Personality and Social Psychology, 61*(2), 195–202.

Schwarz, N., & Clore, G. L. (1983). Mood, misattribution, and judgments of well-being: Informative and directive functions of affective states. *Journal of Personality and Social Psychology, 45*(3), 513.

Seiter, J. S., & Dutson, E. (2007). The effect of compliments on tipping behavior in hairstyling salons. *Journal of Applied Social Psychology, 37*(9), 1999–2007.

Sherif, M. (1936). *The Psychology of Social Norms.* New York: Harper.

Shih, M., Pittinsky, T. L., & Ambady, N. (1999). Stereotype susceptibility: Identity salience and shifts in quantitative performance. *Psychological Science, 10*(1), 80–83.

Shiv, B., Carmon, Z., & Ariely, D. (2005). Placebo effects of marketing actions: Consumers may get what they pay for. *Journal of Marketing Research*, 383–393.

Shultz, T. R., & Lepper, M. R. (1996). Cognitive dissonance reduction as constraint satisfaction. *Psychological Review, 103*(2), 219.

Sigall, H., & Ostrove, N. (1975). Beautiful but dangerous: Effects of offender attractiveness and nature of the crime on juridic judgment. *Journal of Personality and Social Psychology, 31*(3), 410–414.

Simons, D. J., & Levin, D. T. (1998). Failure to detect changes to people during a real-world interaction. *Psychonomic Bulletin & Review, 5*(4), 644–649.

Skinner, B. F. (1938). *The Behavior of Organisms: An Experimental Analysis.* New York: Appleton-Century-Crofts.

Skinner, B. F. (1948). Superstition in the pigeon. *Journal of Experimental Psychology, 38*(2), 168–172.

Snyder, M., Tanke, E. D., & Berscheid, E. (1977). Social perception and interpersonal behavior: On the self-fulfilling nature of social stereotypes.

Stepper, S., & Strack, F. (1993). Proprioceptive determinants of emotional and nonemotional feelings. *Journal of Personality and Social Psychology, 64*, 211–211.

Strack, F., Martin, L. L., & Stepper, S. (1988). Inhibiting and facilitating conditions of the human smile: A nonobtrusive test of the facial feedback hypothesis. *Journal of Personality and Social Psychology, 54*(5), 768–777.

Strack, F., & Mussweiler, T. (1997). Explaining the enigmatic anchoring effect: Mechanisms of selective accessibility. *Journal of Personality and Social Psychology, 73*, 437–446.

Strack, F., & Neumann, R. (2000). Furrowing the brow may undermine perceived fame: The role of facial feedback in judgments of celebrity. *Personality and Social Psychology Bulletin, 26*(7), 762–768.

Strick, M., van Baaren, R. B., Holland, R. W., & van Knippenberg, A. (2011). Humor in advertisements enhances product liking by mere association. *Psychology of Popular Media Culture, 1*, 16–31.

Thompson, D. V., & Chandon Ince, E. (2013). When disfluency signals competence: The effect of processing difficulty on perceptions of service agents. *Journal of Marketing Research, 50*(2), 228–240.

Townsend, C., & Shu, S. B. (2010). When and how aesthetics influences financial decisions. *Journal of Consumer Psychology, 20*(4), 452–458.

Tversky, A., & Kahneman, D. (1973). Availability: A heuristic for judging frequency and probability. *Cognitive Psychology, 5*(2), 207–232.

Tversky, A., & Kahneman, D. (1974). Judgment under uncertainty: Heuristics and biases. *Science, 185*(4157), 1124–1131.

Tversky, A., & Kahneman, D. (1981). The framing of decisions and the psychology of choice. *Science, 211*(4481), 453–458.

Tversky, A., & Kahneman, D. (1991). Loss aversion in riskless choice: A reference-dependent model. *The Quarterly Journal of Economics, 106*(4), 1039–1061.

Valins, S. (1967). Emotionality and information concerning internal reactions. *Journal of Personality and Social Psychology, 6*(4), 458.

Van Baaren, R. B., Holland, R. W., Steenaert, B., & van Knippenberg, A. (2003). Mimicry for money: Behavioral consequences of imitation. *Journal of Experimental Social Psychology, 39*(4), 393–398.

Van Bavel, J. J., Packer, D. J., & Cunningham, W. A. (2008). The neural substrates of in-group bias: A functional magnetic resonance imaging investigation. *Psychological Science, 19*(11), 1131–1139.

Wansink, B., Kent, R. J., & Hoch, S. J. (1998). An anchoring and adjustment model of purchase quantity decisions. *Journal of Marketing Research, 35*(1), 71–81.

Wells, G. L., & Petty, R. E. (1980). The effects of overt head movements on persuasion: Compatibility and incompatibility of responses. *Basic and Applied Social Psychology, 1*(3), 219–230.

White, G. L., Fishbein, S., & Rutsein, J. (1981). Passionate love and the misattribution of arousal. *Journal of Personality and Social Psychology, 41*(1), 56.

Whittlesea, B. W. (1993). Illusions of familiarity. *Journal of Experimental Psychology: Learning, Memory, and Cognition, 19*(6), 1235.

Williams, K. B., Radefeld, P. S., Binning, J. F., & Sudak, J. (1993). When job candidates are "hard-" versus "easy-to-get": Effects of candidate availability on employment decisions. *Journal of Applied Social Psychology, 23*(3), 169–198.

Wilson, T. D., Houston, C. E., Etling, K. M., & Brekke, N. (1996). A new look at anchoring effects: Basic anchoring and its antecedents. *Journal of Experimental Psychology-General, 125*(4), 387–402.

Worchel, S., Lee, J., & Adewole, A. (1975). Effects of supply and demand on ratings of object value. *Journal of Personality and Social Psychology, 32*(5), 906.

Zajonc, R. B. (1968). Attitudinal effects of mere exposure. *Journal of Personality and Social Psychology, 9,* 1–27.

Zajonc, R. B. (2001). Mere exposure: A gateway to the subliminal. *Current Directions in Psychological Science, 10*(6), 224–228.

Zajonc, R. B., Murphy, S. T., & Inglehart, M. (1989). Feeling and facial
efference: Implications of the vascular theory of emotion. *Psychological Review, 96*(3), 395–416.

Zaltman, G., & Zaltman, L. H. (2008). *Marketing Metaphoria: What Deep Metaphors Reveal About the Minds of Consumers.* Boston: Harvard Business Press.